Awakened by Death

Stories of Transformation

KAREN SWAIN

CYRUS KIRKPATRICK

Book One

The Awakened Soul Series

DEDICATION

All our loved ones in spirit who are guiding us while we walk on the earth.

CONTENTS

INTRODUCTION

When I was a young girl going through many of the traumas and dramas within my family, I was given a message. A message which has the potential of ceasing all war, and much of the fear we are living with in this physical world. It is the message the authors in this book have come to know through their own life experiences, and when we realise this message as our truth, life on this planet will be completely different for all who inhabit it.

The fear of death underpins every survival fear we have. Fear of not enough, fear of getting sick, fear of rejection, and on it goes. When humanity realises we are here on this beautiful planet for a short adventure, and after we have finished we will return from whence we came—back to a world of unconditional love and infinite possibility, we may start to enjoy the adventures and challenges we have here in this environment. We will see them for what they are: lessons in expansion and spiritual growth.

In this first edition of **The Awakening Soul Series**, I have gathered together some of the most incredible stories around the experience of death I have come across. As a teacher of deliberate creation, and through my radio podcast show, I have met and had conversations with some amazing souls who have first-hand experience of death in all its myriad of forms.

Some have experience the loss of a beloved child through a terrorist attack or a shooting, some have experienced their own deaths resulting in an NDE (near-death experience,) either from an illness or a medical mishap, and some have experienced different realms of existence; realms that can be places people go when they leave their physical bodies. Further, some have explored all of it in a passionate search for meaning and to alleviate their fears around the death experience.

Some of these topics are controversial. For instance, many people say we do not die until we leave our physical body and don't come back, and so the near-death experience is not what happens when we die, but it's just an out-of-body experience we have to an interim place of our own creation to commune with our guides and loved ones in spirit, to receive a message, or to remember something we need to take back into our lives.

Nonetheless, this book is not about the semantics of if people died or not, it is about the transformation a human personality can experience when confronted with something that has long been believed as the most traumatic experience of our lives—death!

We see death every day on the news, and hear it reported on an hourly basis: The death toll, the tragedy, the terrible horrific horror of it all. Our scary movies are only scary because we believe the very worst thing that can happen is we get killed.

The tragedy of death has been so perpetuated in our society as the worst thing that can possibly happen to us. As a young healer, when I looked out into the world and thought; how can I help? How can I alleviate some of the suffering in this world? I saw that helping people overcome the perceived trauma of death, showing them it is not the ending we think it is, seemed to be the thing that would do the most good. To let people know there is NO DEATH and even though our physical body may cease to exist, our mind and soul live on to explore and experience other adventures in the infinitely vast creations of the eternal reality.

I know you will enjoy the journey we take you on through the pages of this book. We look forward to hearing your comments and knowing how reading these stories transformed your life.

Big Love - KAren Swain

FOREWORD

I was lying on the couch one day stressing about exactly how I was supposed to fulfil my soul plan and make a difference in this world, when my spiritual Guides came through loud and clear: You see, I wanted to make a movie that would tell the world what I had come to know from my spiritual journey and my many experiences with people who had crossed over. I wanted people to receive a message I had received, but I just didn't have the faintest idea how to make a movie, or where the money would come from to do this.

This is when I heard my guides say, in a very clear voice. *"'Oh Just get over yourself KAren, stop stressing and make it simple . . . Just write down what you know. Make this easy, write down your story and let the rest unfold."*

A book, they want me to write a book! I thought. Another daunting assignment, as I had no idea how to write a book either! Writing and reading had never been my strong suit, as I was dyslexic as a child and spent years in remedial reading class, always frustrated at my lack of adeptness in this area of learning.

As I embarked on this writing journey early in 2006, my memories came flooding back. Stories, words and spiritual teachings just poured out of me as my fingers moved across the keyboard. I typed as fast as I could to keep up with the ideas igniting my mind and pounding my heart. This was when my book *Return to Love* was born. Getting the stories down was easy, editing and structuring the book so it made sense took me months and months, as I was so unsure of my ability to write. Because I was a dyslexic child, reading and writing tormented me most of my life, and the thought of being a writer or even knowing how to structure a sentence was something I was very unsure about.

My book *Return to Love*, is the journey of my early spiritual experiences with some of my family and friends who left this world too soon. They contacted me after they left this world to deliver a message, which they repeated to me many times. The book also shares stories from a friend who had an NDE and another who was contacted by her brother at the time of his transition. He came to show her what it felt like to return home to love. In my chapter, I have shared my story about my mother and my best friend and how they showed me this life is but a dream we have from our home in spirit.

Then in mid-2016 my book adventures were to continue as one of my wonderful podcast guests said it would be a great idea to turn my radio podcast show, which is filled with some of the most incredible personal transformative life stories, into a book series. And that critical voice came back again saying: *"I am not a writer and I have no idea how to do this."* Then again at the end of 2016, another friend asked me to join her in a *Chicken Soup for the Soul* type of book series, sharing people's stories of transformation, and how they overcame the many traumas we experience while here on this polarised planet. After an initial halted start (because my friend pulled out saying she didn't have the time to devote to the series.) I again picked up this project early 2017 and set forth asking some of my podcast guests to put their journeys into chapters for the book.

Putting this book series together has not been a smooth journey, mainly due to my writing and reading challenges, but my desire to share what I have come to know has been so much greater than the initial challenges I faced.

This book will illuminate your mind and open your heart, with the many stories of the beauty and love that is our life beyond this life. You will remember the unconditional love our creator has for us and discover a more enlightened meaning to life and death, as you continue your life journey.

The chapters in this book are written by people with extraordinary stories to share. Many of them, like me, are not professional writers; and getting their stories down in writing has been a year-long adventure. I hope you keep this in mind as you read their stories—in our view what is said is far more important than how it is written. Many have never written anything before; and so this was their first foray into writing.

Thankfully, we had the help of the wonderful Cyrus Kirkpatrick, who has edited many of the chapters. Cyrus is also one of the chapter authors, is the author of *Understanding Life After Death* (2015), and he has a group on Facebook called *Afterlife Topics and Metaphysics* which attracts many people looking for answers to the questions of life after death. I was so lucky to find someone who has a knowledge of the afterlife and who could also edit and help put together this book.

What I have found over the years of disseminating spiritual knowledge in articles and blogs, and as I have strengthened my connection with my own intuition, spiritual guides and inner-being, is that writing has become a flow of unexpected pleasure for me; as the words seem to be given to me in a cascade of mesmerising stories, channelings and clear memory recall.

I have loved putting this series together and being a part of spreading one of the most important messages of our time.

The Message

KAren Swain

I was given a message. Not once or twice, but many times dating back to when I was a young teenager. It took me a while to share this message with others, as when I was younger this was not something most people were ready to hear from me, nor was I ready to share with others what I experienced. And life continued to provide me with amazing mystical adventures that really drove this message home.

The questions in me started when I was about 5 or 6 as I watched my dysfunctional family dramas play out. I wanted to know WHY: Why I was in this dysfunctional family? Why do we come to earth? Why are babies born in sin and have to be baptized? And what are we supposed to do while we are here? I used to drive my parents crazy with all the questions when I was a child. Questions they had no hope of answering from their human perspective. My mother would say to me, "Ask your father," and my father would say, "Go ask your mother."

This message came as a response to the many questions I had when I was around 12 and my mother became ill. She had been unhappy for many years, which started way before my dad left her for a younger woman. I first started to think about death and its many implications as I watched my mother suffer the humiliation of her illness and pain. This went on for many years before she eventually left her body. Her journey with cancer, pain, her medical treatments and her death experience ignited many more questions within me about this physical life journey. Where do we go when we die, and if there is a place we go to, where did we come from before we were born? How can we live in a way which would have less suffering, pain and illness and how can we create more connection to our Soul, Health, Love, and Joy?

I have had many experiences with death since I was 15, starting with the death of mum, but also with many other family members and very best friends who left this world way too soon. All of them came to deliver a message. They said it in many different ways, wrapped around many different events in my life, but all of them delivered the same message that kept me seeking answers to life's most perplexing questions about who we are and why we are here.

This is a journey that continues today as I experience an ageing body and bump up against the many misconstrued ideas and beliefs we have been fed about age, illness, disease and death. And as life keeps unfolding, my inner guidance continues to show me how all this living and dying stuff fits together.

All my friends in spirit said the same thing. A message that would alleviate much of the suffering we go through as humans, and change the game on this planet forever at a time when humanity really knows in their hearts the truth. This is a message everyone needs to know, not just intellectually, not just as a fun story in a book, but intrinsically, openly and living through our hearts. This realisation has the potential of transforming our world and the way we live in it.

They said to me: "*I AM NOT DEAD!*"

I feel it is the time we are to share this message more powerfully, and so I do this through the stories of the wonderful people I speak with on my show ATP Media and by sharing my own life story.

This chapter is a look into my book '*Return To Love*,' where I chronicle some of the experiences I have with my mother and friends who died too young, who came to tell me how we are all eternal beings who are here to experience a physical life adventure, and then we return to our true home, back to the love that made us.

From Return To Love

Mum is trying to get through to me.

My mother left this world when I was sixteen-years-old. She passed from her physical body at the age of 50, after suffering the ravages of cancer and chemotherapy. Over the years I dreamt about her many times, especially in my early twenties. She came to deliver a message and in every dream she had the same thing to say to me. She told me this same message in a variety of different ways and in many different circumstances, but no matter where we were, or who we were with, she told me that same thing every time:

She said to me: "*I am not dead.*"

The dreams would start with me discovering her in a strange place, like working in a shop in Queensland, or in a different country, or at a stranger's house. It was always a place where I did not expect her to be.

"O MY GOD! You are here!" I would say to her when I saw her.

"Yes I am here," she would answer.

"I can't believe you are HERE! I can't believe YOU'RE REALLY HERE!" I remember thinking over and over again. "I thought you were dead."

"NO Karen, I am not dead," she always said.

"If you are not dead, then where have you been all this time?" I would ask her, shocked and confused.

The initial shock that she was actually with me after not seeing her for so long would go on for a while. Then, when I calmed down, I would ask her more questions like, "What have you been doing all this time?" "Who have you been with?" "Where have you been living?" "I still can't believe you are here!"

The dreams were always confusing and disjointed as I tried to remember them in the morning. I was interpreting them through my own personal belief system, with my fears and misunderstanding of the eternal life experience.

Anger was the dominant feeling I would remember as I awoke in the morning. If she didn't die and she has been alive all this time, why the hell didn't she want to be with my brothers and me? Didn't she like us anymore? I would think she'd abandoned me after she informed me she didn't die. But as the daylight hours hit my waking mind, I realised it was all just a dream and she was still dead. Phew! She didn't really abandon me. It was all just a dream. As real as it seemed, she was still not here in this physical life.

Dreams are strange and enlightening playgrounds. Our dreams give us messages about what we believe about our waking physical life. In our dreams we live out the thoughts that run our existence. The feelings that dominate a dream show us the type of thoughts we are living with, which attract the circumstances of our lives. If you can remember the dominant feeling you had in a dream, it will surely show you the dominant feeling you have in your life.

These feelings and emotions are the ones that are getting the most attention from the universe. The thoughts or ideas you most indulge in create the balance of the experiences you live, and these situations reflect the feeling you had in your dream. Even when we are not open or willing to look at our emotional set point, our dreams will clearly show this to us. Dreams communicate what lies inside our subconscious mind. One could say it is our inner voice talking to us, or our inner-being guiding us. This is happening all the time, and sometimes our inner voice wants our full attention, which happens at night while we rest. We are being helped while we sleep, as our inner-being communicates to us on every level of our consciousness. The question is, which level will get our attention?

This dream platform is a wonderful place to find answers that may not be available to us during our physical life existence. The physical world around us is truly hypnotic, and it has mesmerised us to the point of gaining all, or most, of our attention. We are so busy trying to control and perfect the circumstances of our lives, and seldom stop to think about perfecting the circumstances of our inner world, our mind.

A death experience reminds us we cannot control or perfect every circumstance in life. Usually it renders us helpless in the face of a circumstance that's out of our control, and this feeling is a feeling so many of us try to avoid. We all want to feel we have everything under control, our destiny is in our hands and happiness is ours to live. When someone does something like dies, it can feed our insecurity that things are completely out of control. Here we all are trying to have a great life by avoiding horrible things, and yet horrible things seem to be unavoidable.

What if we were to view these horrible things in a way that felt better, instead of trying to avoid them? What if none of them were horrible at all? What if we looked straight at them with a renewed perspective and saw them as gifts, instead of horrible dramas? Because the only way to avoid them is to leave the planet and transition back into the pure positive energy that made us.

What were my dreams telling me? Was mum showing me I had a belief that was not serving me? Was she showing me the source that was causing much of the unhappiness I felt in my life? I had felt abandoned by the one person who was supposed to love me the most: My Mother.

This belief played out in a variety of disturbing ways in my young life. My unconscious thought was; if mum didn't stick around to love me, who else would love me? This was not the truth of course, but just one of the many lies I would tell myself to justify why I would push the people who wanted to love me away. The truth was, my Mother came to tell me she did not abandon me and that she did not die. She wanted me to know she was always with me and I could be with her anytime I wanted to. She was trying to communicate to me that I was loved and that I can never be abandoned. I wish I had I understood the dreams better at the time. These types of dreams stopped when I was in my early thirties, when I arrived at a better understanding of how all this living and dying thing works.

After the dreams stopped I had waking visits from Mum a few times. Usually she came to give me a message. Sometimes I would listen and sometimes, when I was so busy with the daily tasks of life, I told her I would call her back.

This day was one of these…

I was in my early thirties and was coming to an understanding that I had always had the ability to tune in and talk to my inner-being and receive the guidance I was looking for. I was now realising I always had a relationship with my inner-self and I could talk to a source of great wisdom, my greater self, and find the answers to my many questions without seeking an expert to facilitate this for me.

At this point I was exploring consciousness in energy healing courses, and had set up shop as an energy healer. I was developing my intuitive and psychic abilities and could now readily communicate with dead people, spirits, and guides. I could also read people's subconscious thought forms and help them overcome their limiting beliefs systems, just as I was overcoming mine. I was coming to a better understanding of how all this living and dying stuff works. My thirst for answers was being quenched; I was listening to my guidance more, gaining a trust in my inner-voice and myself, and coming to the understanding that I did not need all the courses and teachers to teach me what had always been within me. However, such a time of exploration was all a part of my awakening process, showing me what was always there—and I am grateful for all the adventures and courses for that.

It was late on a summer afternoon that I was preparing for a night out with my beautiful little 8-year-old daughter Anika for her Christmas school play. We had a Japanese student, Yumiko, staying with us who was in Australia to learn English. This was a fascinating time in my life, as many more of my burning questions about life and death were being answered, and Yumiko, our beautiful Japanese guest was a very special part of this time.

Yumiko was in her late fifties then, and not your average student living in Sydney learning English. She had a strong desire to come and live in Australia one day. She had worked in the same factory her whole working life, lived in the same house, raised two children, and outlived her husband. Now, late in the game she was looking for a new adventure. We fell in love with her. She was a single mother's Angel, a gift sent to my little family of two. It was like the universe sent me an Angel to look after us, at a time when we would really need it.

Around four o'clock, I took five minutes out of my busy day to have a shower and relax before I set about dealing with the details of the evening. I had so much to do before we took off for the school play. "I will just take five minutes to relax and rest," I thought to myself as I got into the shower. "Just five minutes, then I will rush around like a mad thing and make sure everyone is fed and ready to go."

I sat on the floor of the shower and let the hot water cascade over my head and body. The heat of the water felt so calming and nurturing as I sat there meditating. I love the feeling of hot water running over my skin, I was in bliss. I closed my eyes to enjoy the sensation more, and then…
BANG!

There she was in all her glory. My mother's face in profile. As clear as day, just her face. It was one of the clearest visions I had ever seen. As I stared at her she turned to look straight at me, with piercing eyes and a serious look on her face.

"OOOOOOOH NO Mum! I don't have time for this right NOW!" I said to her. "I have a million things to do! I'm just stealing five to relax before the rush."

I opened my eyes as quickly as I could, trying to rid myself of this psychic experience, but Mum was having none of this. The moment I opened my eyes, many of my other physical senses were engaged, giving me a STRONG experience of her presence.

I could smell her, I could hear her voice, I could FEEL her presence, and memories of her came flooding back.

"OH MY GOD," I said to myself. "I REMEMBER. I REMEMBER YOU."

I could smell her, it was such a familiar smell. I could feel her, I could almost taste her. I looked around me, she was everywhere. I could feel her everywhere. I could feel her and yet I couldn't see her. It was an amazing experience, one I will never forget, and one that has never been replicated to this day with such clarity. It had been about twenty-three years since she had left the planet, but this experience put her right back in the room with me, just as she was when she was alive and being mum.

"Listen Mum, I know you have come to tell me something," I said to her; "but I don't have time for this right now. I have so many things to do and I have to get Anika to school before the play, so she can get ready for her big part. I will call you back, OK!"

As quickly as I could, I leaped out of the shower and raced to get dressed, hoping that my busyness would stop her essence. It did, and we made it in time for the start of the Christmas show.

The festive occasion was wonderful, Anika's dad was there with his new partner and we all enjoyed celebrating Christmas at the school play. Especially Yumiko. It was her first Australian Christmas play and she just loved it! It was a happy night filled with appreciation, laughter and adoration for my funny, beautiful little daughter and her cute school friends all dressed up on stage and loving it!

What was it that mum had come to tell me? Did I call her back? The next morning revealed everything . . .

Kate was my best friend at the time, we did a lot together. She made me Godmother to her first born son Oliver. I even saw him enter this world.

I met Kate working in a pub. She was 18 and I was 19 and had just arrived back in Australia after trekking around Europe with some friends and my trusty backpack. I was wearing the latest bright blue mini skirt and jacket straight off the racks of the Italian marketplace and I have to say, I felt pretty special. She looked me up and down and thought, "Who do you think you are all dolled up like that, some fashion model! This is a pub not a catwalk."

I too had my critical opinion of her. A tall slender country girl, not afraid of anyone, out there and open to the world with an air of country confidence. The sort of un-abrasive fearlessness only country people have. Innocent, trusting and very brash. I judged her straight away.

She was different to most of my eastern suburbs private school friends. I was very wary of her, but in awe of her brashness and jealous

17

that I didn't have that kind of confidence. We stared at each other for most of the day trying to size each other up. She was working in the public bar with all the diggers and I was serving people in the bottle shop in the next room.

The bar extended into the bottle shop, so I could see her every move. Kate had so much confidence with the patrons, laughing at their pathetic jokes, and ignoring their leers. She had a strong, long lean body and everyone who met her admired her beauty, including me.

The next day she asked me if I wanted to have lunch with her. We bought takeaway and sat in the main bar, which was shut during the day. She dared me to put a song on the jukebox, but I thought I would get in trouble from management. Exasperated with my wimpish lack of adventure and courage, she waltzed over to the box and put on 'Let's Dance' by David Bowie. We kicked up our heels and danced all lunch, trying to outdo each other with our high kicks.

We partied together, argued over boys, wore each other's clothes, loved and laughed. I loved every minute I spent with her. She was such a hoot, so brave and daring. She would challenge herself to do outrageous things. Things I never dreamt of doing. Other people's opinions did not stop Kate from enjoying her life. She loved life like no one I had ever met before.

She told me when she was a small child she would see people standing around her bed in the middle of the night. She was scared of them, not understanding what was happening to her. She thought they were there to take her away. So every morning that she was still alive and kicking, she would thank the universe for giving her life. She told me that she was so grateful and happy every day to be alive.

I had never heard this sort of thing from anyone in my life before. I was in awe. I had never met someone that loved life that much, who felt so happy just to be alive. As you can imagine, armed with this attitude she manifested everything she wanted out of life at a young age.

Kate came from a middle-class country family. Her father liked his drink a little too much, and would often spend the household money on booze at the club. Her Mother was not happy about this, and if you ever met her, she would tell you. In fact that's all she had to say most of the time. How hard life was, what a dead beat her husband was. The complaining would go on and on, but this never seemed to dampen Kate's lust for life. I was amazed!

We were the best of friends, we went through many joys, trials and tribulations together. But something happened to Kate when she was in her mid to late thirties that she found difficult to deal with, and her lust for life had left, leaving her struggling with a darkness and depression she found difficult to overcome. I will not go into her story in detail here, but you can read more about her in my book **Return to Love.**

The morning after Anika's Christmas play the phone woke me. It was my ex-husband. We had been with him the night before, so I wondered why he was calling me so early. What did he want when he could have asked me only hours before?

"Have you heard the news?" he said to me.

"What news?" I said impatiently.

"So you haven't heard?"

"What! What is it that I haven't heard?"

"No one has called you this morning?"

"NO! NO one has called me this morning! What are you on about?" I screamed at him.

It was early and he was doing the *Guess What I Know* game on the phone. I was not impressed.

"Sit down. I have something to tell you. Kate is dead," he said, "she was found yesterday around 4 PM."

This was around the same time my mother came to visit me in the shower. I knew Mum had come to tell me something, and I am glad I didn't listen at the time; as it would have spoilt my night at the Christmas play. I will never know how she was going to tell me because I shooed her away, but I knew she had something important to say.

I was so angry with Kate. How could she leave me again? We had been apart because of a misunderstanding, and we were back in each other's lives now, so how could she leave me AGAIN? But she never left. In fact she had much more to tell me after her transition than in the months leading up to it.

One of the last conversations I had with Kate was only days before she left her body. In previous conversations we had together, I tried to get her to focus on her life in a more positive way, and to get her to appreciate herself again. I told her a truth I had known for a long time. I said that she was a healer and a teacher and she had a lot to offer the world. Her normal passionate and appreciative attitude about life was such a joy to be around. I told her that people needed to know what she had known about being so appreciative for being alive. People needed to hear about her and learn from her example.

She had always known the secret to achieving the life of her dreams. Her **attitude of gratitude** for being alive, her passion and her love of life had brought her everything she had dreamed of at a young age. She had achieved her Cinderella story because she didn't make her simple childhood circumstances the reason to feel bad about herself. Even in the face of my rich snobbish private school friends and their judgments of her, she always thought of herself as lucky.

She listened and tried to feel what I was saying as I talked to her about how important she was to me, and the people around her. But she was determined to be right about how she was all wrong!

Then just days before she left the planet, while we were in my kitchen, she asked me something. She came very close to me and held her hands up to my face with her palms facing me.

"Do you really think I am a healer, KAren?" she said to me. "Do you really think I have healing hands?" she repeated as she thrust her hands in my face.

I stepped back not quite knowing how to respond. This was the first time she had said something positive about herself in months. I was shocked and a bit confused.

"YES" I said abruptly. "You are a healer, of course you are a healer."

Little did I know at the time how this conversation would play out after her transition.

Life Beyond Life

I spent a good while being angry and pissed off at Kate after she transitioned, and when the anger subsided, I cried, a lot. I couldn't believe that she was not here anymore. I had plans for us, and she was not going to be around to fulfil them. I stopped seeing clients because I was in no state to help anyone. I was the one needing the help this time, and I received it.

Yumiko, our Japanese student, was like an angel sent from heaven. She nurtured us, did our washing, cooked our dinners and totally looked after me and my daughter while I was going through my anger and tears.

I was so lucky to have her there to help us. "Did Kate, or the universe, plan all this?" I thought to myself.

I knew Kate was happy now. I knew that she was not suffering in any way now that she had returned home. I knew that the despair she had suffered in the last year of her physical life had completely been erased, now that she had reemerged back to her eternal self. I knew she had returned to the pure positive energy we all come from and she was viewing life from this expanded eternal perspective and had all the knowing of the universe. I was not crying for her, I was crying for me. I wanted her back, I wanted my friend back. Even when she was depressed and totally self-absorbed in her own dilemmas, I loved being with her. I loved her so much, and I still do.

The love that I felt for her in the months after her transition was overwhelming. It was as if someone had turned the volume up full blast on the love and appreciation I felt for my dear friend. I talked to her every day. I screamed at her and asked her a thousand questions. But when she first left I was not in the emotional or vibrational place to hear her reply.

Kate's body was on ice for over a week, and by the time of her funeral I had calmed down. I wanted to see her body. I wanted my young daughter to see her too, so she could say goodbye, something that still haunts her today. I didn't know if this was the right thing to do—to subject a small child to a dead body. But I felt it would help her at some stage in her life to have had the experience. We are all going to leave the planet one day, and I wanted to demystify the experience of death for her.

I saw my mother's body in the coffin on the day of her funeral and thought it was fascinating. I could swear I saw her breathing, I thought I saw her chest moving up and down as I watched the vessel that had once inhabited the spark that I knew as my mother. I guess I wasn't used to seeing a body lay perfectly still.

When we arrived at the funeral home I asked the attendant if Kate looked okay. "She looks beautiful," she said. "Are you sure, because I am taking my small daughter in with me? She doesn't look too scary?" I asked her again.

"She looks very peaceful and beautiful," she replied.

My daughter and I walked in together and saw the coffin at the end of the room. At first all we could see were some clothes and hair poking out the top of the coffin, but as we drew closer we had full view of the bodily remains of my beautiful friend. There she lay as still as ice, and as cold. It was a huge shock to both of us, and we burst into tears and ran to the back of the room to sit down. We both gasped for breath and held each other tight. It took a short time but when we had calmed down, I asked my daughter again if she was sure she wanted to see Kate's body.

"Yes, yes," she insisted. "I want to see her, I want to see." A curious little being just like her Mum.

We walked slowly back up to the casket and cautiously peered in again. This time it didn't feel so bad.

We just stood there staring at her, not quite sure what to say or feel. She had on one of the fabulous outfits she had designed in the last years of her life, and she looked wonderful; however, her make-up looked very scary. It was if the person who had applied it had forgotten to bring their glasses to work that day. I joked with her about it. She wouldn't have been seen dead with such a bad make-up job.

After a while we became more adventurous and tempted to touch her body. It was ice cold and rock hard. My daughter was fascinated by the whole experience and started to ask me all manner of questions about life and death. She was receiving the experience of death as another part of the life adventure, not as the sudden disappearance of someone she once knew and loved.

We stayed for quite a while; both of us felt a sublime comfort being with Kate's physical form again. Then I started to think of what other people had said to me about their experiences with the dead bodies of the ones they love. Some of them had said to me they felt the essence of the person was not there anymore when they looked at their loved one's discarded form. The body was just an empty shell that didn't even resemble the person they had known.

I closed my eyes, breathed deeply and relaxed. I wanted to feel if this was what I felt. I wanted to have my own experience of Kate's transition, and not be influenced by the memory of someone else's experience. As I stood there in the room of her coffin and her discarded form, an overwhelming sensation swept through me. In my relaxed state, I could feel her everywhere. I could sense her, breathe her, even smell her.

The memory of being in her presence came flooding back to me, but now it was different. Now her presence was somehow bigger and more alive than it had been before.

No, the essence of Kate's being was not confined to her body now. She was not as I had experienced her when she was in her physical body. But I definitely felt her with me. I could feel her strongly and everywhere. She was no longer in this body before me but she was most

22

certainly there. As I stood in the room with my eyes closed the memory of being with her grew stronger and stronger. Her essence, or energy, felt so big – so much bigger than the body lying before me.

This presence, this enormous energy that I recognised as Kate, was not inside the body anymore. She was so much more than the personality I had danced with in life. My experience of her was no longer confined to her physical form.

Now I was inside her! I was inside a huge energy that seemed to stretch beyond the boundaries of space and time.

I didn't want to leave; it felt so good to be in that room in her enormous presence. I felt her inside me, above and below me. She was everywhere! She didn't say anything to me at this stage, or if she did, I didn't hear her in a legible sense, but I could feel her beautiful omniscient presence, and this gave me great comfort. I walked over to read the lid of her coffin, which was leaning up against the wall and noticed her middle name was Rose.

I had forgotten she was a Rose.

Kate was with me all the time during the months just after her passing. I dreamt about her every night. It was as if she was waiting for me to fall asleep and awaken into my astral body while my physical body slept, so we could hang out together again. When I left my physical focus, and lifted out into my non-physical focus, I would see her sitting on the end of the bed waiting for me to reawaken.

Of course her passing was the talk of the town, everyone had something to say about it. None of the friends I grew up with and who knew Kate would understand what I was going through with my communication with her after her passing. I tried to tell them, but they were not interested. They told me they didn't believe in the things I talked about, so I stopped talking to them about my experiences.

Then one night I had a very vivid dream. I was in a room with a group of my friends and just like in life they were all talking and gossiping about Kate's death.

"She didn't die, you know," I told them.

"Oh Karen, how deluded you are, of course she died," they said to me.

"No, No she didn't," I said. "There is no such thing as death," I told them, "She lives on in another place."

"Poor Karen, she is in denial," they said to each other and continued to gossip.

I broke away from the group feeling left out and not heard. I could see that no matter what I said they would not hear me, nor did they want to. As I turned my head away from the group I saw a brilliant light coming from a doorway in the next room. I went over to investigate and when I reached the open door I saw the room was filled in a brilliant white light. As my eyes adjusted to the brilliance, I saw Kate's body lying on a white chaise lounge.

"Is she asleep or is she dead," I thought to myself. So I started to walk slowly over to the lounge, staring at her trying to figure out if she was asleep or dead. She looked so very still. "Maybe I am wrong," I thought to myself. "Maybe my friends are right, she is dead and I am making all this life after life thing up. Am I just trying to make myself feel better by making up silly stories that are not true?" I wondered.

As I continued to walk slowly closer to the lounge, I became more doubtful of myself. "She definitely looks dead," I thought as I stared at her motionless body. I reached out ever so carefully to touch her. Would she be cold and hard, or is she just sleeping? As my hand drew closer to her face, almost at the point of touching her cheek, she abruptly opened her eyes and stared at me. I drew my hand back with a start.

"OH MY GOD!" I said. "You scared me. I thought you were dead. You definitely looked dead, but you're not, you are still alive, you are still here!"

She smiled at me with the reassurance of someone who knew the answers to everything. "I AM NOT DEAD" She reminded me.

"You know everyone is talking about you, everyone thinks you're dead," I told her.

"I know Karen; I know they think I'm dead. They don't know, they do not understand; but you do," she reassured me. "You know."

A life-changing experience.

We were with each other a lot back then. I don't dream or feel Kate so much these days, but I can tune into her anytime if I want to chat. One of the nights we were together, Kate gave me one of the most vivid encounters I could have ever hoped to have of the life after life experience. I had been reading a lot about life after life and had many questions about where we go and how it all works.

My friend gave me the best experience and understanding I could have asked for. She showed me in a very real way that we live on eternally, and I will always be grateful to her for that. Truly she is my teacher, healer and best friend.

Not too long after Kate had left the planet, as I awoke into my nightly focus, I saw Kate sitting in a comfy chair across from my bed. As my mind adjusted to the scene, it felt like she had been sitting there waiting for me to wake up. How strange this was, because what I was actually doing, from this perspective, was falling asleep.

I sat on the edge of the bed and Kate walked over to join me. As we chatted I had this epiphany about the fact that I was actually with her. Our life together and our relationship was continuing as if she had never left.

"This is amazing," I said to her. "You really are NOT dead, are you?"

"***No. Karen I am not dead***," she reminded me with a smile and a cheeky look.

"I just can't get over this experience I am having with you. I am actually with you. You really are here with me in the flesh, so to speak. I can see you, I can touch you. I can talk with you

and I can hug you if I want." SO I gave her a big squeeze.

"You really are here aren't you? Really and truly!"

She smiled at me again with a reassuring look, and we reveled in the joy of this realisation that we are all eternal beings.

It was fascinating to me to have this experience of life after life. I was in a reality that felt more real than most of my waking physical life. My other life, the one where I had been to her funeral, cried and screamed about her passing and even stopped seeing clients, felt like a distant dream to me in that moment.

We talked about it as if we were talking about a dream we had had together. Kate really had not gone from my life at all; here she was right in front of me, talking to me as if nothing had happened!

"Had I made it all up? Was the other life where she had died been a bad dream?" I thought to myself, while having this sublime experience.

As I recall, in this non-physical experience, we were sitting in my bedroom, but it was very light. I remember it looked like a pure white environment. We talked about what everyone was going through in the earthly experience. We talked about the confusion that was felt throughout her friends and family. I wondered why more people didn't

25

have the knowing I was sharing with her. Why they were not open to remembering this type of experience.

She told me she had been with others in their nightly existences, but they were not available to remember the experience because of the sadness they felt when they refocused back into their physical life.

While I was with Kate my physical existence became the dream, an illusion I was creating with my mind and thoughts, and the experience I was having with Kate was my true reality. I felt very comfortable and at home while I was with her. This place, even though it looked like my earthly

bedroom, felt more to be my home than my physical house address.

It is an experience that will stay with me always. Truly, this feeling of belonging and remembering has been a wonderful gift. I had read in the books like *Illusions*, *Conversations With God* and other spiritual books that this life was an illusion that we are making up with our thoughts and feelings. Now I had been given this experience of really understanding and feeling my true existence. An existence of pure joy, elation and LOVE.

What a relief it is to know that nothing that happens to me in this earthly experience can change the pure love that is here for me, that is me, and that we all can return to. Truly this was a wonderful gift, and a life-changing experience, knowing no matter what we encounter while we are here on earth, we can all return to Love, in the body or out of it.

About KAren Swain

KAren is a Teacher of Deliberate Creation; Spiritual Channel and Mentor, Founder of Blissful Beings, Reminders from Home, Writer, Podcast and Radio Host of Accentuate the Positive Media; Founder of The Awakening Soul Series, and Author of Return To Love and How Can I Get What I Want.

KAren enlightens you to the power of your thoughts and beliefs, how they create your world and how to live in alignment with your emotional guidance system. KAren is one of Australia's Foremost Thought Leaders and Change Agents, Showing you the way to a Happier Healthier More Connected Life.

Services: Personal Sessions, Seminars/Webinars, Festivals and Media.

www.karenswain.com
www.karenswain-atpmedia.com
www.theawakeningsoulseries.com

We Don't Die:

Discovering Who I Am by Believing in the Afterlife

Sandra Champlain

"Who am I? What is my life for? What happens after I die? Is Heaven real?" are all questions that I believe are normal for humans to ask themselves. As children and young adults, we live life in the present moment and do not think about these questions. However, as we get older and especially after we experience loss, these questions may come to the forefront of our minds. You are reading this book so there's a great possibility you are in that place of wonder.

For me, I was thirty-years-old looking at the stars one night, when my mind started asking those questions. Of course, there were no answers available within my own mind. When my mind was quiet those nagging questions kept appearing. Not finding answers, my mind started to play out the worst possibilities; answering such questions with, "Sandra you are no one, your life doesn't matter, you simply cease to exist when you die and there is no such thing as Heaven."

This repetitive message was in my mind so often that I developed an incredible fear of dying. Thankfully, this fear led me on my quest for knowledge and answers. Twenty years later I have my answers, I am at peace, and am so grateful I can share my journey with you.

Let me start with talking about our minds. Firstly, my mind is no different than yours. As humans we start life believing that everything is possible. We are excited to live life, explore, and we don't want to take naps or go to bed early. We dream of growing up and being a teacher, an astronaut, the president, or anyone we wish. Then, for some reason the ego or "The Voice" (what I call it) is born. It is that negative voice that says things like, "I'm not good enough" or "I'm not special" or "I'm stupid." It becomes a constant companion during our journeys here on earth. As I tell you my journey, I ask that you consider your own voice. You'll notice that it rarely mentions all of your accomplishments and successes. It is always looking at what is unfinished, where we have failed, and pointing out our negative traits and behaviors.

One of the messages my voice had told me was to not trust anyone. I was that little kid that eagerly waited for Santa Claus, the Easter Bunny and the Tooth Fairy, and I can remember when my beliefs in them were shattered. Over the years, I became a skeptic. I didn't trust anyone and I had to see it to believe it. I remember hearing about a local psychic when I was a child and my parents telling me, "Psychic abilities are not real." My skeptical mind threw the world of spirituality in the same waste basket as Santa Claus.

As I began my search for proof of the afterlife at thirty years-old, I can see how my skeptical mind tried to convince me that I would not find any answers. They say that people do things for one of two reasons - to avoid pain or to move toward pleasure. My fear of death and unanswered questions were the pain that motivated me to begin my search, regardless of what my skeptical mind told me.

I was raised Roman Catholic and heard great stories from the Bible and was told to have faith. Unfortunately faith didn't help stop the fear. Instinctively, I chose to study many of the major world religions. I thought that perhaps one of them would hold answers to my questions. While I did find incredible stories and wonderful inspiration, no religion had the proof I needed. I assumed there was no answer to be found and chose to try not think about the fear. However, when someone says, "Don't think about a purple cow," what do you think of? A purple cow. I thought about fear.

Months went on and my uneasiness about life and death continued. Then one day, I was introduced to a weekend seminar held worldwide called The Landmark Forum. The seminar promised concepts like success and power. I loved taking this weekend course because it answered so many personal development related-questions and gave me insights to the negative voice in my head, plus the power to not listen to it. However, there was another important benefit to my journey, as well—I met a new friend named Nance.

Nance was a nurse. She was fun and I really liked her. However, she spoke of spiritual topics like angels, psychic mediums and life after death. I tried to be open and not let my opinions from the past dictate my beliefs.

The two of us went to see a medium do a stage show. My mind was filled with notions that it was all an elaborate set-up to swindle people out of their hard-earned money. It really is difficult for me to stop the skeptic in my mind! However, after witnessing beautiful, precise messages this medium had for people in the audience, I couldn't help but think, "This is real."

I had to know more about this medium and lo and behold, I found that she offered a weekend course in mediumship. Secretly, I attended the course and was hoping to find some credible evidence in the afterlife to rest my fears. There are no words that could have prepared me for the experience I had the very first day. The instructor told us how psychic mediumship happens, how we are all made of up energy, and that energy can never be destroyed after the body dies. She told us that as souls we keep our personalities and can still communicate through thoughts.

To demonstrate what happens during a medium reading, she asked us to pretend we were mediums. We all found a partner and sat knee to knee. She asked that one of us go first and close our eyes. We were to imagine a safe, highly energetic white light around the two of us and ask for a deceased loved one to step into this light. She told us to use our imaginations to invent a person standing behind our partner.

With my eyes closed I pretended that a man was standing behind her and told her about him. I made up that she had a grandfather with her, he was her mother's father. I said his name was Jan, that he was a fisherman in Denmark and had a big gap between his front teeth. I continued that he had died from lung cancer and he had the regret of never telling his daughter that he loved her. His message was for this woman to deliver an apology and an "I love you" to her mother.

It was fairly easy for me to invent a person and as I opened my eyes, there were streams of tears running down my partner's face. She told me that every word fit her grandfather! His name was Jan, fisherman from Denmark, died from lung cancer and was a tough man, never telling his daughter that he loved her. I was absolutely shocked. I believed I created all of this in my imagination! My partner then turned to me and gave me the name of my grandfather, told me about the cane he walked with and the German shepherd by his side. All of it was accurate.

As the weekend course progressed, I learned that we need to have a healthy imagination for our mediumistic abilities to be present. I noticed that when I felt fearful it would not work. It only worked during the times I was willing to pretend and to play. After experiencing that course, the fear around death was gone.

I chose not to tell anyone about my experience because I was afraid of what people might think of me. I have spent so much of my life bad-mouthing and ridiculing people who believed in "woo woo spiritual stuff" that there was no way I was going to tell anyone that I became one of those people. However, I kept having the feeling that a lot of people would benefit hearing my story. Secretly, I continued to explore what other evidence of the afterlife was available and found many great things; yet fear was once again apparent and now it caused me to keep my mouth shut.

Many year passed until January 2010. This was the year my father was diagnosed with cancer. Only a few months later, on May 11th, Dad took his last breath. I wish I could tell you that it was an easy time for me and that my belief in the afterlife kept me going, I cannot. Perhaps you have experienced it as well, the loss of someone you love so dearly.

The pain was so severe before and long after his death. My healthy relationship with my siblings became one of those awful stories you hear about - fighting over everything. Things got so bad that not only did I lose Dad, but I lost the relationships I had with them.

To put things into a bit more perspective - my grandmother had passed away before my father, then my dad died resulting in the relationships with my siblings dying, as well. Then suddenly my cat Ozzie had to be put to sleep. Combined together, I was in the deepest, darkest period of my life. I was not considering suicide but I had compassion for anyone who felt the way I was feeling and could understand why they'd feel that was their only option. I felt like I traveled with a dark cloud over me. I experienced more tears and body aches than ever and could not imagine life ever getting any better.

Thoughts entered my mind one day, "Is this all a part of grief? What is grief? Why does it have to hurt so badly?" It dawned on me that everything I was experiencing must be a part of the grieving process. I turned my attention to investigating grief and this process. I was looking for answers and answers I found!

Grief is nature's way of our brains and body adjusting to a new reality. Anytime we have a significant loss, we grieve. Not just the death of a loved one, but we grieve when we lose a relationship, a job, our health and many more scenarios. I looked into brain chemistry and found that there are neurotransmitters associated with grief. Anytime we love or have an attachment there are brain connections established. The more we love the stronger these connections are. If you can imagine someone addicted to a drug you can imagine how strong the attachment is in their body and mind. When we take away the drug what happens? Withdrawal. Have you ever seen someone in withdrawal? It is not pretty. Their body and mind aches for that substance, they have physical and emotional pain and their minds are not clear.

Love is like a drug. When a person we love dies we go through withdrawal as well, it is called grief. As with the drug addict, it takes the grieving person time for the brain chemistry to balance itself again.

When I studied grief I had an "ah ha" moment. I realized that losing our healthy neurotransmitters during grief has many side effects. Besides the pain, the tears, the anger and the sadness, our neurotransmitters control our sleep, our memory and our perception. I learned that those grieving may not see reality as it is actually happening. I felt that the arguments I had with my siblings were about things that did not happen in reality. I had an instinct that none of us kids had enough of the healthy neurotransmitters and it wasn't a matter of me being "the greedy sister" but that everyone was in such deep grief, we couldn't see what was actually happening. Would we take a drug addict at his or her word while witnessing them in withdrawal? No, we'd wait for it to pass knowing they are going through a tough time. I found out how many families come apart and divorces happen often during grief and realized that people don't have compassion for the pain we are going through during the process.

I didn't realize it at the time but I was transforming in this process. Interesting that it is only when we look back on a period of our life can we see it as a gift. Moments of pain have the ability to give us some of our biggest life lessons and awakenings. Instead of being a victim of my own grief I had the opportunity to share what I knew with others. I was discovering that the way to get peace for myself was to help others who were hurting as well.

I knew I had to share these life-saving words with as many people as I could. The thought "write a book" came into my mind but the voice in my head told me I was not smart enough. Late one night while scouring the web for advice, I read, "The world is waiting for your words." Deep inside I knew people would benefit from what I know. As helpful and as lifesaving as the grief information was, I knew how much my life had transformed when I found the reality of life after death. I also knew my book would be titled, "We Don't Die."

I attended a weekend seminar about book writing, called "Author 101 University." I didn't have the courage to share with people there what I wanted to write about. I remember the fear running inside me. There were several hundred other attendees and when people asked me what I wanted to write about I simply said, "Grief."

I spent the three days of the course taking good notes but at the end headed for the door knowing that I'm no author. Just before I exited, a man greeted me and asked me if I got everything I wanted from the seminar. I responded, "Yes"

He asked "What do you want to write about?"

In my mind, I could actually see a fork in the road. If I told this man a lie I could see the road leading nowhere and being disappointed in myself. As scared as I felt in that moment, I told him that I wanted to write about "life after death."

This man turned out to be the publisher of Morgan James Publishing, the company that organized the seminar. He invited me to sit with him and talk about the book I wanted to write and why. My voice was shaking, I had tears in my eyes but I told him the entire truth. As he listened he appeared to be amazed and asked, "Do you really think you can write a book like that?"

I said confidently, "Yes."

My homework was to write a book proposal. I had to state what the book was about, why it needed to be written and why I was the person to write it. He asked me to write two chapters that would be my best information for readers. He assured me that I didn't have to use big words, I just needed to write like I was talking to one person.

This man had the belief in me that I didn't have in myself. I always find it so interesting that our views of ourselves rarely match what other people think of us. Inside I've often felt like a nobody, certainly not smart, a failure at times, not attractive and not so lovable. What does everybody else think of me? Family and friends would use words like lovable, generous, successful, creative, confident, independent and fun. During my awakening guess what I have learned? They are right! Same goes for you my friend. The outside world sees us for who we really are while our inner critic tries hard to convince us that we are less than that.

I hustled to complete my two chapters and my book proposal. I learned about all the pain and anguish in the world caused by death and grief, I learned of the divorces and all the suicide. I gave that book proposal everything I had and Morgan James chose to publish me!

I held my book for the first time in October 2013 and I was delighted! Those closest to me knew I was writing a book, but I still had so much fear about what others would think. Again I experienced another awakening! I was so fearful that people would think of me negatively for being interested in the afterlife and the opposite happened each and every instance. Most people have experienced the loss of a loved one and questioned life and death. Instead of being thought of as a weirdo, I was embraced by people.

My transformation continued. I became the confident person people saw me as and less and less did I believe the negative thoughts coming from my own mind. I wish I could say I am perfect, but I am not. However I did a little research on what confident people do and chose to adopt some of their strategies. For one thing, I keep learning and stay in communication with those who speak the same language (as in, sharing the same interests). I have a taken spiritual courses and even started my own radio show. It is very difficult to be down in the dumps when I regularly am reminded by people that I am a soul having a human experience! I also have a personal coach who asked me to create a "vision statement." This man only talks to me as the powerful woman I say I am.

I'll share my vision statement with you and encourage you to write your own. It is a roadmap for me and helps me put my life in perspective when times get tough.

Sandra's Vision Statement

"I am perfect just the way I am. I have been created in God's image. Everything that I may feel is a struggle or imperfection, is actually a gift to me. All humans are perfect, experiencing their own opportunities for growth as I am experiencing mine. One of the opportunities I picked is to learn to love myself exactly as I am.

Times that I believe to be tough are the times that I receive the greatest growth for my soul. Every experience I have becomes a gift that I can share with a fellow human being so that they may have a better life. Daily, I am gaining mastery how to be kind and loving, to myself and others, no matter what the circumstances.

I love my life and I know that I am responsible for my happiness. Everything in my life is here because I requested it... because there is good that comes from it. Every situation, every relationship is a learning experience to me and others. I have learned to see the gift in everything, where in the past I may have made things wrong.

I appreciate all that I have and all that I do. I stay in the present moment and fully experience my life through the 5 senses and my emotions.

The work that I do is in perfect harmony for what I am up to in the world. Every person I come in contact with makes a difference for me or I make a difference for them. I am grateful for all the relationships I have. I love and appreciate all the people in my life and they love and appreciate me. I surround myself with powerful, positive and fun people. We nurture each other, stand for each other's greatness and empower each other to succeed. Love, respect and joy are present in every relationship.

I am ok with the unknown. I can live happily and in peace even in times of uncertainty. Although I may not understand how the events in my life are going to turn out, I trust that everything is for my own benefit. I trust God and the Universe that my life is unfolding exactly the way it is meant to be.

Fear exists in my life as a challenge and a game. I realize that fear is normal and that I cannot ever really get hurt. I live by my motto that "We Don't Die" and as real as fear may seem, I know that it is only an illusion. I take daily steps through my fears and know that on the other side of fear lies a miraculous, abundant, fun-filled life.

I love and appreciate my body and mind. I treat my body with love and respect, giving it the whole, natural foods it craves to keep it strong and healthy. Sunlight, fresh air and being out in nature are as necessary to me as they are for all life on earth. I enjoy exercising my body regularly and love the feeling of a strong heart, strong lungs and strong muscles. When my body feels strong, my mind feels strong.

I exercise my mind regularly. I enjoy reading and learning and playing games that keep my mind sharp. I know that my mind is a tool and I consciously create my thoughts. I don't allow myself to listen to negative self-talk. I know that they are just automatic thoughts that I do not have to listen to. Like changing a station on the radio, I easily can change my self talk to a positive station or turn the radio off and have a quiet mind allowing me to receive creativity and inspiration. I purposely turn my channel to gratitude and empowering thoughts that lead to me taking powerful actions, which give me fabulous results.

I have true purpose. My life is for me to learn, to grow, to love, to forgive, to experience, and to share all of that with my fellow traveler. My challenges and obstacles sometimes lead to success and sometimes lead to lessons of self forgiveness, self-love and self-acceptance. I have the privilege of sharing my journey with others. I inspire other people to go after their dreams, because I go after mine. I inspire people to be courageous, because I am courageous. I inspire others to love and believe in themselves because I love and believe in myself. I inspire others to live knowing that life is an education for the soul, because I believe life is an education for my soul. My true satisfaction comes when I can help or inspire another person. I am excited in the morning of each day knowing it will bring great things. I go to sleep every night feeling love for myself and so grateful for the difference I make."

As you may realize, it is hard to feel like a victim of circumstances after reading that!

I am not perfect and neither are you, we are human beings, my friend. There is no right way or wrong way to do life. Times that we suffer and hurt the most are the times we can have the greatest transformations and they can be the biggest gifts. It might not feel it at the time but can you look at your life and see some of the hardest periods and how you have grown as a person because of them? If I can give you one piece of advice for your journey it would simply be to help your fellow travelers any chance you get.

Zig Ziglar said it best, "You can get everything in life you want if you will just help enough other people get what they want."

Silver Birch said "Service is the coin of the spirit."

I want to end this chapter being of service to you so that you may have knowledge and resources to fully believe in life after death. I truly believe if you don't have the fear of dying you won't have the fear of living life to the fullest. If you believe your deceased loved ones have survived and they'll be right there to meet you when you close your eyes for the last time, then you won't need to grieve. You can believe that they can hear you, see you and even give you signs from that invisible place they live, which is all around you. I really do believe the Hereafter is literally that. Here, in the present place you sit, just after the body is gone. Remember, energy can never be destroyed. We cannot see the wireless internet around us or television signals to know they are real. Trust me, Heaven is in that same space. Quiet your mind and believe and your life will be filled with miracles.

(You can find Sandra's resources, the 19 Reasons to Believe in Life After Death, at the end of this book.)

About Sandra Champlain

Sandra Champlain is the author of the #1 international best-selling book , "**We Don't Die** - A Skeptic's Discovery of Life After Death" and host of "We Don't Die Radio." She is the subject of the documentary film, "We Don't Die." Sandra is a keynote speaker, a member of the Afterlife Research and Education Institute (afterlifeinstitute.org) and empowers people globally to live their lives fully.

sandrachamplain.com
wedontdieradio.com

Hit By A Truck

An Atheist Visits Heaven

Nancy Rynes

My life seemed pretty quiet during the autumn of 2013. I was an artist and science writer with a comfortable, predictable job, a supportive family, and plenty of good friends. But while I liked what I did for a living, after almost 20 years of it I wondered if I might need a change in my life.

Something about my life wasn't feeling right to me even though I couldn't pinpoint anything specifically that wasn't working. Somehow, I felt that I was on the wrong path and out of alignment with who I was at my core. I didn't really know what to do about my uneasy feelings, so I let them slide and got on with daily living.

Early December of 2013 came and with it, bizarre dreams that kept me from sleeping soundly. These dreams were very strange, colorful, beautiful, and yet disturbing in some way that I didn't understand. My sisters and a few friends thought they had mystical significance, but with my background and career in the sciences and technology, I wasn't quite open to those "woo-woo" explanations. I was on the fence about God, spirituality, and an afterlife. I didn't truly believe in God, and certainly not the God of my Roman Catholic upbringing. I wanted to believe in something greater than simply physical reality but never saw any evidence of it. Being in the sciences for over 20 years I learned that if I couldn't touch or measure something, it didn't exist. Therefore, God and all things spiritual didn't exist, at least in my thinking.

A few weeks after those dreams started, my whole life flipped upside down. A simple bike ride to run some errands led to almost everything in my life changing in a heartbeat. The most profound change was my outlook on matters of Spirit.

January 3, 2014, was a date that brought in sunshine and warm breezes to my home in Colorado. A longtime cyclist, I appreciated being able to ride outside all year in my state. Since the day was just about perfect, I decided to run some errands around town on my bike. My body was a little out of shape from taking the previous month off riding due to injuries, so I planned a slower, shorter outing than usual.

Riding south from my home, I felt physically strong, alert, and glad there was very little traffic. At just shy of a mile from my starting point, I cautiously rode into a new traffic circle that recently replaced a three-way intersection. It was difficult enough to navigate in an automobile so I used extra caution as I rode into it on my bike.

Once in the traffic circle, I continued riding south in the designated bike lane. A small car followed me but stayed far behind. Some vehicles approached on the road, coming in from the right but I didn't worry too much since they appeared to be slowing down to stop before entering the circle.

As I began to cross in front of the incoming traffic, it appeared that the driver of the lead vehicle, a large SUV, saw me and was stopping. A split second later, though, I realized she was driving straight into the traffic circle without even slowing down.

Panic gripped me. I knew, without a doubt, I was going to be hit and thought I would likely die. The odds of a cyclist coming out alive in a confrontation with an SUV were pretty low. Thoughts of my daughter, sisters, and niece flashed through my mind. I tried to steer my bike to avoid a crash, but I couldn't get out of the SUV's way fast enough. The roundabout was narrow, and I didn't have much room to maneuver.

The SUV continued into the traffic circle without stopping and hit me broadside, impacting my right leg and ribcage. Then, by some crazy acrobatics I still don't understand, I ended up on the SUV's hood and looking through the windshield at the driver. It appeared that she was holding a cell phone in front of her on her steering wheel, but I couldn't be sure with the brief glance I had.1

I couldn't find anything to hold so gravity slowly pulled me down to the front of the SUV. Without understanding how I got there, I soon found myself clinging to the front grille, hoping against hope that I wouldn't get pulled under. Time seemed suspended as the SUV continued to drive.

After what seemed like forever, I lost my grip on the SUV's grille and fell to the pavement, my helmeted head and left shoulder hitting with a pair of loud cracks. The terror that I would be run over almost paralyzed me. By a stroke of luck, I somehow retained consciousness, which turned out to be one of the things that saved my life.

As the SUV pulled me under, my sternum caught on its transfer case. At the same time, I reached up and grabbed the axle with my right arm. The vehicle still moved and dragged me with it, but at least by holding on I wouldn't be crushed by the rear wheels.

Then I noticed something very odd: my consciousness was in two places at once.

I didn't think much about it at the time except "Wow, that's weird." But later, even today, I still find it difficult to wrap my brain around that experience of dual-consciousness. My training as a scientist couldn't provide an explanation for it, but the experience felt so strange that it stuck in my memory.

It seemed like the animal or survival-focused part of my consciousness stayed under the truck in my body, hanging on to the axle, whimpering, and trying not to get run over. That part of me was all about fear, raw emotion, and survival. But another part of my consciousness watched the whole accident unfold from out in front and to the side of the SUV! How could this be?

While this "observer" was definitely me, she did not feel any panic or fear. Her state of being was calm, thoughtful, and loving. She felt she was witnessing something sad but also something that was supposed to happen in the way it was unfolding. The observer-me knew everything would be OK, so why be frightened? I've come to understand that this

---

1 Witness accounts verified that the driver of the SUV appeared to be texting for the several hundred yards before she hit me. While she was initially charged for this offense, plus three others, the District Attorney's office dropped the texting charge due to difficulties in obtaining enough proof to convict.

"observer" was what some would call my soul-consciousness or soul-body.

I had this dual sense of consciousness for what seemed like hours but in reality was only a few minutes. After the initial impact, the SUV dragged me for approximately 50 feet under the vehicle before the driver of another truck was able to stop her. After the SUV finally stopped, I laid under it with the "animal-consciousness" part of me quietly screaming that it wanted to get up and run away as fast as possible. When I began my struggle to move, a searing pain ripped through my pelvis and lumbar spine. I screamed again, this time out loud, then collapsed back to the pavement in fear and frustration.

Still wanting to flee but not being able to move much, I managed to wiggle enough to get my head and shoulders to a point where they were out from under the front of the SUV. Just then, a blonde woman, a pony-tailed angel, ran up to me from my left. She knelt down and said her name was Ann and that she was a trauma nurse. She laid her hands on my shoulders and gently told me not to move.

It turned out that this simple gesture saved me from becoming a paraplegic and I am utterly grateful to Ann from the depths of my soul. She stayed with me until the first responders arrived, then moved off to the side while speaking with me to keep me calm.[2] In a rush, first responders converged on the scene. Several firefighters pushed the SUV away so the paramedics could stabilize me for the trip to the nearest trauma center.

Once the SUV was moved, the paramedics surrounded me. Only then did both parts of my consciousness merge back together. One moment my consciousness was in two separate places and in the next, both parts were back together in my broken body. I didn't feel or experience anything unusual. I simply noticed that "I" was back to being in one place again. The inkling that something very mysterious and perhaps even spiritual had just happened to me flashed through my mind, but it was still too raw and confusing for me to fully understand.

---

[2] Only one other person saw and interacted with Ann, one of the police officers, and the nurse said that she didn't want to give her name. The officer briefly spoke with her after my transfer to the hospital, then Ann disappeared into the crowd. The District Attorney's office attempted to locate her for several months, but all of their attempts failed. I still don't know who she is, but in that moment she was my guardian angel.

The paramedics loaded me into an ambulance and stabilized me as quickly and gently as possible. A blessedly short trip to the trauma center brought me to the ER where the medical team worked to determine the extent of my injuries.

After many tests, scans, and evaluations, a surgeon and the hospital's trauma team came to my bedside in the emergency room to explain my injuries. The good news: I miraculously suffered very little bruising or scrapes on my body, which surprised everyone.

The bad news: I had a major concussion with bleeding apparent in my brain, a broken left collarbone, five broken ribs on my left side, bruised ribs on my right side, minor internal bleeding in my pelvic region, a minor crack in my pelvis, a cracked sternum, and many compression fractures. My vertebrae shattered and burst apart in my lower back, causing many more fractures up and down my spine.

In total, at least 24 of my bones suffered breaks, some in multiple places so it was impossible to determine an exact number of fractures. The majority of the fractures were in my spine, with the most immediate problem being a shattered L1 vertebrae. When that vertebra burst apart in the crash, sharp bits of bone lodged in my spinal canal and were dangerously close to severing my spinal cord. I was still within a millimeter or so of being a paraplegic. That made me sit up and take notice, so to speak.

However, an even bigger shocker was that my neck injuries were so severe that I was close to being paralyzed from any one of them, too. While it hurt less than my back, the fractures and ligament damage was so traumatic that any ill-timed movement could cause the damaged vertebrae to shift out of place and sever my spinal cord. I was hovering close to being a quadriplegic. That sobered me more than anything else. The thought of my legs not working was terrible enough, but the possibility of having my entire body paralyzed was more than I could bear.

The trauma team then installed a hard, semi-permanent, plastic brace around my neck that they said would be my constant companion for the next three months. "Great," I thought. But at least with this on, my neck would heal completely given enough time.

My most damaged vertebrae, the first lumbar in my lower back (L1), would need stabilization as soon as possible. To do that, the surgeon would install titanium rods from the T12 vertebrae (12th thoracic, just below my ribcage) to L2 (2nd lumbar, toward my pelvis) to take the pressure off the burst vertebrae, allowing everything to heal. The titanium rods would stabilize my spine and, in time, those three vertebrae would fuse together and effectively become one large bone.

I spent the next two days flat on my back in an intensive care unit (ICU) room while my body stabilized enough for surgery. Friends and family graciously sat with me through those terrifying moments when I feared my very active life was over. Their visits warmed my heart and soul and their love and support kept my mind on the goal: surgery on Monday, then healing.

* * *

Most people don't look forward to Mondays. I usually counted myself in that group, but this day was my first step in getting my mobility back so my impatience could not be held in check.

I have never liked going under the knife. Three prior surgeries years before left me a little skittish about the anesthesia. I hated the forced loss of consciousness and, like many people, always had that nagging fear of not waking up.

My surgeon and his team arrived to explain the actual procedure in more detail. The surgery itself would last about two hours and the medical staff expected me to achieve a full recovery in 2-3 years after the vertebrae healed. Eventually, a nurse wheeled me into the operating room where the surgical team prepped my IV and anesthesia drugs. The anesthesiologist joked about it being time for cocktails, then I drifted off.

I have had three previous surgeries that required the same general anesthesia as I was getting today. None of those experiences were remarkable in any way. In all of them, the anesthesiologist gave me the drugs, I drifted off into a gray state of nothingness (I wouldn't call it "sleep"), and what felt like the next second I was waking up in the recovery room. 3 No memories, no dreams, no sense of anything happening, just the experience of slipping into a gray unconsciousness one second and waking up in recovery the next.

Not this time.

---

3 If you haven't been in surgery, having anesthesia may seem odd and unfamiliar. It's not sleep. It's really a state of unconsciousness. It's characterized by lack of memory, lack of pain, and muscle relaxation (wikipedia.org). You don't dream.

I did drift off as the anesthesiologist gave me my "cocktail," but it wasn't to the gray state of nothingness that I expected. I didn't realize it at the time but my body reacted badly to the anesthesia, causing my heart rate, breathing, and blood pressure to flatline for 2-3 minutes. While the surgical team fought to pull my body back from death, I had no sense of their frantic attempts at resuscitation. Instead, I found myself standing in a spectacular landscape unlike any I'd ever experienced. Warm breezes drifted across my skin. Beautiful vistas of meadows and distant mountains surrounded me. And a pervasive, loving presence overwhelmed me in its intensity.

My mind tried to wrap itself around what was happening since it felt so real. In the back of my awareness, I knew I had just gone into surgery, but I wondered if I had somehow dreamed the bike accident and my injuries. This place felt more real to me than any on Earth.

Around me was a landscape of gently rolling hills, flower-filled grassy meadows, towering trees taller and grander than any here on Earth, and a sense of a light mist floating through the air as if it were a humid summer morning. The sky gleamed a very light, pearly blue, similar to what you might see at the ocean's shore, with wispy clouds and a very bright but somewhat diffuse light.

Below the surface forms and colors of the landscape, I somehow saw or sensed vibrating energy. It seemed I could see the surface of a leaf, for example, yet also see below it to an energy-level; a vibration of love or compassion or kindness that made the leaf take on a subsurface radiance. Everything had this radiance: trees, grass, sky, flowers, and clouds. Colors seemed intensified by it. And a feeling of love flowed through everything and heightened this underlying energy.

Through it all, I sensed and somehow physically felt an incredibly profound feeling of peace, rightness, goodness, and love flowing through my body. I cried, literally wept, at how beautiful it all was and thought to myself that it was definitely an OK place to be during my surgery; much better than that gray nothingness I had expected. I didn't know where I stood or how I came here, but I felt at home, right, and at peace.

The beauty I saw and felt in those first moments really does deserve a capital "B." It wasn't just pleasing to the eye, but there was something deeper to it, more harmonious, more blessed, and more powerful. Everything felt tied together by an enormous amount of love and peace. Somehow I knew that the beauty of the landscape around me was the product of unconditional love on a cosmic scale.

I didn't know how it was possible to feel love as if it were a physical presence or energy, but I did. My being vibrated with love to its core. Love-energy flowed around me like a gentle current, washed through me, and eventually captured me by the heart. I felt supported by a Divine Presence so powerful, yet so gentle, that I cried again. I had never experienced such unconditional love and acceptance in all of my years on Earth.

I began to wonder if I died on the operating table, and if I had died, why was I here in what seemed like "Heaven"? I didn't believe in any of this stuff! I didn't believe in God, or angels, or an afterlife — why was I here? Shouldn't I be in that "other place"?

The answer came back not through my ears but in my heart. "You are my child. This is your home. Welcome home." With that simple statement came another wave of pure, unconditional love. I wept. I was loved, even though I hadn't believed in any kind of God or Divine Presence for most of my life. I was welcomed back home where I belonged, welcomed back to the reality of Spirit.

Soon, a figure in a human-like, female shape appeared to me. She approached silently, coming in to view as if emerging from the mists, and greeted me with an energy-embrace of pure love.

This being wasn't recognizable as someone I'd known from my life. I wondered if she was a spiritual teacher or guide of some kind, sent to bring me to whatever comes next. I hoped that was the case — I had already fallen in love with the place and wanted her to help me stay there.

Kindness, compassion and caring radiated from her I felt that she held that deep love for me in a way I had never experienced before from anyone. Not romantic love, but a love you might expect from an angel, a saint, or the Creator. This love felt completely unconditional and fully accepting.

In hindsight, being able to feel love and energy flowing through me seems strange. After all, it's not what we humans normally experience in our own lives. We touch with our skin, hear things with our ears, and see with our eyes. But the only things we typically feel are our own internal emotions, discomforts such as body pain, or other physical sensations. We feel heat or a chill through our skin, but as humans we don't typically feel love as a physical force.

But in that place, love felt like a normal, physical force.

My visitor never did tell me her name while I was there, although later, as she continued to visit me in my hospital room after I returned to my body, she said that I could call her Mary since it was a name that she had used at one time. Mary also asked me to avoid getting too wrapped up in her name, saying, "It's simply a name, and many women have been known as 'Mary' over the millennia." What mattered to me at that moment in Heaven was that she acted as my mentor and guide during my stay.

Mary strolled with me through the landscape. We marveled at the flowers that vibrated with colors that I can't describe in human words. Trees formed a canopy overhead, pearly sunlight filtering through the branches. I enjoyed walking, feeling healthy again with no pain, sensing the cool grass beneath my bare feet and the warm breezes on my face.

In time, as I grew more comfortable in her presence, Mary began telling me more about this place. I wasn't in Heaven per se, just in a place to prepare me for what was to come — a slice of Heaven you might call it. I was in the waiting area. Heaven's green room.[4]

A glimmer of hope that I'd soon see the real Heaven sparked in my heart. If this was the waiting area, just imagine how amazing the full experience of Heaven would be!

She went on to explain that she chose to be a voice to me from many others beyond where we were now. I got the impression that these were spiritual beings who somehow communicated to me through her. I somehow knew that these included God, the being we call Jesus, and many spiritual masters and teachers. Mary was a representative of sorts, a speaker; one who came here to help me start on the next part of my journey.

She began communicating information to me, messages or lessons that those in Heaven wanted to pass along to me and others back on Earth. These teachings were concepts that Spirit suffused them with constantly; knowledge that was an innate part of this place as it was beyond here. These messages contained knowledge that many of us on Earth seem to have either forgotten or never learned but were an integral part of existence in Heaven.

Mary communicated to me that the messages were initially intended for me so that I could improve my own life. I was being given the opportunity to make my own life one that I truly wanted to live. Eventually, they were also meant to be shared with others, to help others who were on a spiritual path.

---

[4] Even though I actually visited a "pre-Heaven," for clarity's sake, I will use the term "Heaven" through the rest of the chapter.

She explained that in the past, I volunteered to serve by being a messenger of these teachings. At some time, perhaps before I was born into my present human life, I had apparently made an agreement to serve light and love in whatever way Spirit thought best. Mary actually placed a vision in my mind of this happening, a vision from her perspective as a witness. I stood with others in a light-filled room and agreed to be a kind of messenger. But I still had a hard time believing that I somehow made an agreement before I was born. How could that happen? What if I changed my mind didn't want to do it?

Mary told me that souls often agree to different kinds of tasks before they are born into a life. Some tasks are small in scope, and some, like Nelson Mandela's, are large, but they're all voluntary. I volunteered for my little task of being a messenger of these insights to as many people as needed to hear them.

She made it clear that now was the time where I'd be fulfilling my part of the contract. But since it was voluntary, I could also decide not to follow this calling. I wouldn't face anger or retribution if I walked away from the task.

A very palpable sense of the weight of responsibility overwhelmed me. Even though it felt a bit overwhelming, I wanted to do this at a very deep level. I wanted to help, both myself and others.

My lessons with Mary kicked off.

We strolled again through the landscape as she communicated many things that the spiritual beings in that beyond wanted me to understand.

Sometimes she talked, passing on information as you and I might talk as colleagues at work. Other times the communication was more spiritually-based. These spiritual communications came to me as feelings, visions, and impressions straight into my mind and heart. Sometimes I simply felt a sense of immediate knowing, other times I experienced feelings and visuals mixed with words. This non-verbal method of communicating seemed strange at first, but it didn't take long before it became natural.

The messages she passed on to me encompassed the basics — Spirit 101 is my term for them. She, and those who spoke through her communicated to me the nature of love, community, gratitude, companionship, how we're all connected spiritually, that we're never alone, and so much more.

Early in my tour of Heaven, while Mary and I lingered on that first hillside overlooking the distant mountains, she gave me something very precious. She gave me a glimpse into what Spirit and Heaven felt like to her. Looking into my eyes, she somehow shared her mind and soul with me. For a few moment, I felt what it was like to be a spiritual being.

As I melded with her, my mind seemed to expand beyond anything I can describe. I felt a deep connection with many other spiritual beings, and I could see those connections at an energy level: little gossamer threads of loving energy, of connection, coming in to me from many unseen souls.

I felt the deep connection to Divine love, and the constant communication with God that permeated Heaven. And I experienced something else, something that startled me. I felt Mary's allowing of Spirit to take care of everything. She didn't fight the flow of love and wisdom coming into her from the Divine. She simply relaxed spiritually and allowed Divine energy to flow into her and to work through her. No angst or fighting for control. Simple allowing.

Mary, and the beings who communicated through her surrendered to the Divine flow of love, peace, knowledge, and connection. They didn't struggle, they simply allowed. Once I had experienced this deep connection and allowing for myself, she severed that connection and gave me back my sense of individuality.

One of the strongest visuals Mary gave me during my time in Heaven centered on the power that we have in the choices we make. It came as we walked along a creek in a little valley that wound among some ancient-looking, worn down mountains. I gazed at the mountains and trees, enjoying the peaceful scene. Then we came upon a small pond. Its water was dark and deep, and a few colorful leaves floated on its surface. Mary instructed me to kneel by the water's edge. When I did, I sensed this wasn't an ordinary pond. She asked me to touch the surface gently, and see what would happen. Well it was a pond, I knew what would happen, but I followed her instruction anyway. By now I knew simply to do as I was told.

Ripples emanated outward from the place I touched the water. The leaves moved up and down in response to the ripples that moved under them. But superimposed on the ripples, I saw the choices that I'd made in my life. Those choices, like those ripples, made little waves in the world around me. They affected other people. They affected my future.

And they somehow affected my past, too. Good or bad, my choices had an impact.

I saw how the choices I made impacted others, not just from my own perspective but from theirs, as well. Mary allowed me a glimpse inside of the people with whom I had interacted in my life. I felt their hurt when I inadvertently hurt them. I felt their happiness when I was kind. I felt their sadness when something I did negatively impacted them. And I felt their gratitude when I reached out to lend assistance.

This was my life review, although it was so subtle that I didn't understand what it was for over a year after my NDE.

Mary continued to guide me through the landscape, teaching me about love, gratitude, connections to others, community, creativity, and much more. After what seemed like 2-3 months of teaching me, we wandered into a meadow. She surprised me by laying down in tall grasses, inviting me to join her like little children would, staring up at the sky looking for animals in the clouds. She seemed to be trying to help ease my fears a little by interjecting some lightness and play. It worked. We stared up into the shimmering cobalt blue sky, watching the clouds drift by and giggling like little girls. We were simply friends out enjoying the warm, sunny, summer day and gazing up into the sky looking for rabbits and dragons and horses. I had some moments of fun staring up into that beautiful, shimmering blueness, trying to name shapes that came and went as quickly as a breath.

Spotting cloud animals in Heaven — what fun! I assumed that a spiritual existence would be all seriousness, solemnity, and stern faces but she allowed me to see how playful, loving, and joy-filled it could be.

Eventually, she rolled over onto her side, then rose to her feet and said, "I need to go soon, and it's time for you to get back to your life."

Panic and anger flared through me. I did NOT want to go back. Heaven was too amazing, too supportive, and too loving for me to leave. A part of me desperately wanted to stay in spite of the commitment I had to keep.

Grudgingly, I allowed her to help me stand. Mary stayed firm in her stance and insisted that I had accepted a mission that I had agreed to go back to Earth and serve others by passing along these teachings.

She explained that she would help me a little before she sent me home. She performed what I now know was a healing of my soul-body. Her hands paused over some of the areas that were most painful in my physical body and she sent loving energy into the wounds.

50

When she finished her healing work, she looked at me and said, "It really is time for me to leave now. And it is time for you to go back to where you belong". I opened my mouth to argue again, but I suddenly awoke in a bed in the recovery room, confused and sobbing.

* * *

My time in Heaven continues to work its magic of transformation in my life. When the nurse rolled me into surgery I was an atheist, but I came out a true believer and spiritual seeker. It wasn't easy to have my entire world-view turned upside down in such a short amount of time, though. A few friends bowed out of my life after I went public with what happened when I died in the operating room. I understood and allowed them to back away, wishing them love and peace. I did mourn those losses, even as the NDE brought new friends into my life.

Some part of me, the "old me" kept trying to deny the experience altogether though, thinking that living the rest of my life might be easier if I just ignored being in Heaven. Fortunately for me, this internal struggle lasted only a few months. I realized I was happier and more loving by accepting my NDE as real so I relaxed, allowing the experience to begin to transform my life.

In the first few months after my experience I did face challenges with daily life on Earth. I felt deeply disconnected from God, Mary, and the other spiritual beings who helped me in Heaven, but the most heart-rending struggles I faced were in seeing the sometimes-horrible ways we treat each other and this planet. The violence, hatred, drama and simple struggles of daily living overwhelmed me at times. I'll be honest – these struggles still pop up in my life, but instead of allowing them to batter me, I choose to take a different vantage point. They are opportunities for growth for me, for other people, and for society as a whole. I have chosen to focus much of my personal spiritual practice, and many of my talks and workshops, on these societal pain points—thus using them as tools for transformation.

My life makes more sense and flows more easily when I live the truths God, Mary, and the others gifted me with during my NDE. Living the gifts of those teachings from Heaven helps me stay calm, loving, centered, present, peace-filled, spiritual, and happy. The old me often wallowed in fear and anxiety, shunning love, connection, and community. The "me" that I am now is the "me" I was meant to be: loving, calm, fearless, peaceful, and connected, and all of it thanks to the lessons I learned in Heaven.

I spend much of my free time being of service to others. This was a rare occurrence for the pre-NDE Nancy but now, I feel a deep sense of joy when I give my time and expertise. One of my current projects is growing food for my local food bank. This is a community and family affair – my daughter is involved, as are several families from the city in which we live. Not only are we serving others by helping to feed those facing economic challenges, but we're creating a community "in spirit."

I learned so much from my NDE that it's impossible to pick one teaching that supersedes the others. What tends to happen is that one of Heaven's teachings may be more prominent for a time, giving way to another when I need to relearn its wisdom. Right now, the most prevalent message that I am working with is the power that comes in letting go and letting God work in your life. It's a tough lesson for many people (especially me!), but I find that when I allow space for God to work in my life, amazing things happen.

In time, I learned how to re-establish an incredible and supportive communication with Mary, Spirit, and several of the angelic beings who formed part of the background of "others" in Heaven. After being back in contact with Heaven and living the truths taught to me while I was there, I realize that I am happiest when I am acting as a source of Divine love, writing about spiritual topics, and teaching others what I learned. I continue to author books, write magazine articles, speak, and give workshops about how each person can bring a little bit of Heaven to their lives on Earth.

I have a daily spiritual practice, but in reality my entire life is now my spiritual practice. And I love it!

Life shouldn't be all seriousness, struggle, and self-improvement though. One of the things I took away from my experience is to enjoy my days on Earth as much as I can. I hope you do, too. Have fun! Spend time with family or friends. Laugh and enjoy yourself. Be grateful for what you do have rather than worrying about what you don't. Pay attention to the little things such as how you treat others, the words you use internally, and making time for quiet every day.

The world is a big place with many problems that you can't fix, so try not to dwell on them. Instead, shift your gaze. Focus on what you can do to bring your life, or the lives of others close to you, more in alignment with love and peace. Make these small, positive changes in your own life and realize that when you do this, positive energy flows from you into the world. Yes, you can help to change the world by bringing joy, peace, and happiness into your own life first.

Do what you love to the best of your abilities. This is one of the ingredients for an inspired life.

Listen to the callings of your heart, for in them are the keys to happiness and fulfillment. Your heart-voice is one of God's ways of speaking directly to you.

And finally, know that there is more than just this life, that Spirit is there for us any time, and our time on Earth is precious and wonderful.

About Nancy

Nancy Rynes is a speaker, artist, and author of the books *Awakenings from the Light* (available from amazon.com) and *Messages from Heaven* (available at NancyRynes.com). Nancy's books and workshops teach you how to bring a little bit of Heaven to your life on Earth. She divides her time between Boulder, Colorado and Olympia, Washington.

The Girl with the Frangipanis in Her Hair

Dave Byron

There's not a day goes by that I don't think of Chloe. Every morning when I wake up I have an important decision to make: I could think of the tragedy that unfolded in my life, and this would leave me tripping over my jaw all day; or, I could think a happy thought, and I have so many happy memories of Chloe. Life's too short to keep wallowing in all the bad stuff. If you're going to get on with life, I figure you have to make a decision how your life's going to be, so you might as well make it a good one.

I suppose I came to this because I was sick of living with so much wallowing. Everywhere I went I was seeing people going backwards, and that was me, I was one of them. I had nowhere to go, I blamed everybody and everything. I was lost in the misery and everything was dark. There was just no light in my life, and my daughter wouldn't want that. I had to think about what she would want. I wouldn't want that for her and I know Chloe, she wouldn't want me to stay in my misery either!

G'day, my name is Dave Byron and I like to speak straight from the heart. So I suppose I better tell you my story. I am married to a beautiful woman Tia, and together we had two wonderful children: our son Jared and daughter Chloe. We live in Sydney, Australia near the famous Bondi beach. The third ramp is the place we loved to surf. My daughter Chloe's nickname was *Cloney* down the beach because we were so alike the two of us. We are beach people, we love the surf and we love Bondi, but we also loved going on holidays and Bali was one of our favorite places to go. We loved everything about Bali, the people, obviously we loved the weather, the surf and also the care-free attitude, and so we went there for holidays because it's so laid-back. It was so lovely, we really enjoyed it.

In 2002 for Chloe's 15th birthday I gave her a trip to Bali and she was ecstatic about it. And not long after, I gave her mother a trip for two to Bali for her birthday as well, hoping she would take me. She didn't have to take me, but she said she wanted to—so there we were, the three of us were off to Bali.

It was a great holiday, it really was. Half a dozen of Chloe's school friends, aged between 13 to 15, were also in Bali on holiday with their parents, and we tagged along with them sometimes, which was fantastic. During the day the girls hung out together, which was really great.

Chloe and I surfed together every day, because the other girls didn't surf. After we'd hang out with all the other kids and they would tease me as much as they could. Like, I would go to the fridge for a treat, I usually had some chocolate muffins or a big box of Maltese's in there, and everything would be gone. All the kids would pretend to be asleep on the lounges and I would be like, "Where's all the chocolate?"

Chocolate was smeared all over their faces, on purpose, and they'd yell out, "Come and see us!" It was all so much fun.

I was the third wheel, well that's how Chloe saw it. When I walked down the street holding my wife's hand, Chloe would walk in front of me and slow right down so I had to stop, and my wife would keep walking so I would have to let go of her hand. Then Chloe would grab my wife's hand and this left me walking behind both of them. So I would have to skip in front and slow down to block Chloe and try to get ahold of my wife's hand again. We did it every day. It was just so much fun.

Everything between Chloe and I was a contest. We played table tennis every morning at the hotel. I use to play a lot when I was a kid, so I could play well. I'd let her get really close to winning, really close, then I'd win! She would run down the stairs yelling, "In the pool, I'll race you to the pool." And so it was a race to the pool, then a race in the pool and a race back up to the room. She always won that race to the pool. She had so much laughter and joy about her.

It was the best of times, it truly was, and when our flight was overbooked and we had to stay an extra night on the island, we thought this was a gift from God, another day in paradise. Chloe hung out with all the girls the next day, and my wife and I went jet-skiing. It was fabulous.

It was Chloe's school friend Ashley's fifteenth birthday, and Ashley's mum asked us if it was OK if she could take Chloe out with their gang at night to celebrate her birthday. She assured me that there would be no alcohol. They were going to a nice restaurant and then they would go to the Sari nightclub so all the kids could have a dance on Sari's famous dancefloor, and we said "That's fine, of course."

My wife and I had dinner that night across the road so we could see them. Over dinner we were sitting across the road looking at them, and they were having the most fun you had ever seen—there were all these girls, and they were laughing. I yelled out in a really big voice so Chloe could hear me across the busy Bali street, "Wahini!" which is Hawaiian for "beach girl" or "surfer girl." I loved to call her that.

Chloe spun around and saw me, then all the girls spun around and saw me too, and they all were waving and laughing. Chloe put her head down with embarrassment, it was so funny. All the girls were over there going, "Dave, Dave, we've got chocolate!"

And I yelled back, "I don't want your chocolate." Then I sat back down and my wife and I continued with our dinner. It was so much fun.

It turned out Wahini was the last word I would ever say to Chloe.

Originally I wanted to go to the Sari nightclub first. I wanted to wait till they arrived, but my wife said, "We can't do that, we've gotta let her go."

And being the protective father I am, I said, "Ah no, but it's a nightclub, and . . . we can go and just sit a couple of tables from them so we can watch them."

She said, "No Dave, we have to let her go, she is with all her friends and you can't do that." So I said "OK then, we won't go."

We finished our dinner and walked in the other direction past their restaurant. All the girls were yelling out "chocolate muffins" and waving at me as I walked off.

It was around 10pm, which was pretty late for us, so we went back to the hotel and straight to bed. The phone rang at approximately 11:45pm. My first thought was: they are in trouble—they all had some drinks and got themselves into trouble. I knew this would happen.

I picked up the phone and it was Ashley. She asked if Chloe was there. I said "No darling, Chloe is with you."

"No she's not." She said.

Once again my mind was going in another direction and I assumed she'd run off with someone somewhere. Then Ashley told me there had been an explosion at the night club, and she was at the Hard Rock Hotel with her family.

I said, "Hang on, what's happening?" And she started crying. I got straight up and started getting dressed. My wife Tia asked me what was happening. I gave her the phone and said "You talk to her" and I kept getting dressed. Tia quickly put the phone down, got dressed, and we both ran outside.

We looked down the street outside the hotel towards Kuta and all we could see was a ball of black smoke. I don't know how it was blacker than the night, but it was. It was shooting straight up in the air and there was flames, just like a blow torch, and it was red and orange and angry and violet, spewing into the heavens this awful flame.

We just knew that's where we had to go—but we didn't know how to get there. Then we saw a guy sitting on a motorcycle across the road, so we grabbed him and told him to take us down there. We gave him a handful of money and told him to get another one of his friends, and he did. They put us on their motorcycles and we took off towards the Sari nightclub.

There was a massive amount of traffic going the opposite way. It was human traffic, no bikes or cars. People were screaming and running in the opposite direction. We pulled up to the nightclub—rather, what was left of it, and it was just a horror show. Actually, it was worse than a horror show, it was a nightmare come to life. There were a couple of fire engines and the firemen were doing their best to get hoses working as everything burned. It was just horrible.

We got off the bikes when they couldn't go any further, and we pushed our way through the crowd. I was holding Tia, my wife's hand, but the closer we got, the thicker the crowd became, and Tia couldn't pass. But no one was going to stop me from getting through. I turned around to see Tia's face in the crowd but people moving in the opposite direction pushed us apart. She looked up at me and said, "Find her, find Chloe."

"I'll find her." So I took off towards the nightclub.

I jumped onto the back of a part of a broken vehicle and I jumped off the bonnet into the nightclub (I found out later that it was the vehicle that the bomb was in.) I went into the nightclub and I could see firemen everywhere. I noticed their boots were smashed and cut, and I realised that it was from all the debris on the ground, everything was broken. Everything everywhere was sharp. However, this fact didn't bother me, I was on a mission. I just kept going fast paced as I went into the nightclub.

The further in I got, the quieter it became. Flames were shooting up in the air, but there was no noise. There was bits and pieces of people, limbs, dead people and shattered people. I get flashes of this sometimes. Everything in there was dead. Burnt people and half-burnt people and people with no faces and no eyes, with arms missing.

It was then that I heard the worst thing I've ever heard. Amidst this quietness I heard a girl whisper, "Help me, I'm hot." When she said "hot" she then expelled some air, and I realized that it was her dying breath. I couldn't find her, I looked and I pulled bodies out but I just couldn't. I couldn't tell male from female—that was the extent of the injuries in there. All this damage done by these fucking people, but my overriding thought was: I had to find Chloe, I had to keep going, so I did.

I went around to the seaside where I saw all these Balinese people lined up and they were just standing there dumbfounded looking into this bombsite, not a sound out of them. I was calling out for Chloe. People were running around the corner outside the club, so I thought I would follow them. I walked behind all these people as I continued looking.

Two young guys were sitting near a wall in board shorts and singlets holding each other crying. I think they looked 18 or 19. I went to assist them to see how they were doing and I asked, "Boys, you ok? I'm looking for my daughter." I started describing her but they couldn't stop crying, so I gave them a shake. They weren't even moving, they were just sitting there. I gave them an even harder shake to pretty much snap them out of it. I had to find Chloe—I couldn't have someone crying at me. I said "Listen I've got things to do here, you have to step up here."

One of the boys said, "You don't understand, we were in there when the bomb went off, we were in the garden and we all heard the bomb at the front. A fireball started coming towards the back of the nightclub where we were. They were throwing people over the back wall, mainly the girls as they couldn't get over, but it just got too hot." Both the boys had been on top of the wall helping, but they had to get off as it was too hot. When they did, all they could hear was the screams of the dying who were burning on the other side, and they could do nothing to stop it.

They were putting their hands to their ears saying how they couldn't stop hearing the screams.

Please God, I prayed Chloe wasn't one of those girls who died on the other side of the wall. There was lots of praying to God that night. I had a lot of fights with him too, because I couldn't believe a tender loving god would let something so violent happen. How could you possibly let that happen?

I went through the nightclub again and again, and it was always a similar story – everybody dead. We came out the other end, when I remembered Ashley said she was at the Hard Rock Hotel.

There was a guy at the end of the bomb site sitting on a 650 Harley Davidson dressed in a leather vest with his motor running. He had a kid about 9 with a damaged leg on the back, and as I walked by him he asked if he could help me. I said "Mate, I am looking for my daughter, have you seen any young girls around?"

He said he saw two girls coming out, so I started to describe Chloe, and he said, " I'm not sure, I knew they had long hair.

"I'm going to the Hard Rock Hotel, have you got any idea where that is?"

"It's a long way. Jump on the back and I'll drive you." God puts people in your path to help you sometimes. I jumped on the back of the Harley and I put the kid on my lap and we took off at 100 miles an hour. We pulled up to the Hard Rock in minutes as opposed to half an hour considering it was 4-5 kms away. So yes, God does put people in your path.

When we arrived at Ashley's aunt and uncle's hotel room, Chloe's distressed friends opened the door and hugged me, and I hugged them back. The girls had escaped through a toilet window when the bomb went off. They couldn't stop crying, so I was trying to calm them down, but Candice's aunty was screaming and crying—and I was thinking please, you are not helping these girls by doing this. She was distressed about her sister, and her husband was trying to calm her down, but she just wouldn't. I wanted her to shut up, because all she was doing was keeping the girls upset.

I gave her a paper and pencil. She said, "Why did you do that?"

"I want you to write down everyone's names who was at this party. Ask the girls who was at the party, adults, everybody." She said she could do that, and it finally shut her up. But in reality, none of us knew what to do.

An Australian former rugby league footballer, Craig Salvatori, was staying at our hotel and we'd got to know him. Tia and I saw him pick up his two younger daughters and walk back to the hotel while we were having dinner, so we knew he would be there, but his wife had stayed behind to have drinks with her friends and the rest of the gang—which meant she would have gone to the nightclub. I thought the next thing to do was go to Craig and see if anyone had come home. I pretty much ran back to the Malastia which was very far away. Everything was quiet now on the streets—there was no one anywhere.

I knocked on Craig's door and the door creaked open. Craig, who played front row for Australia, was a giant of a man with a massive head. He popped his head out from around the door and asked me why I was knocking at that time of night.

I said, "Mate I just want to know if your wife is home?"

"What's that got to do with you, what do you want my wife for?"

"Look I'm really sorry but can you come out here." I could hear the kids in the background. "If you just step out . . . I just gotta tell you something and I don't want your kids to hear it."

"I'll step out alright." He wasn't happy. So he steps out into the hall and closes the door behind him.

"There has been a bombing at the nightclub, and I'm just wondering if your wife was home and if Chloe was with her." I said to him I saw Ashley and Candice and then I told him about the bombsite.

"Let's get down there now." He said.

"There is no point, I've been there, gone through it three times and there is nobody alive. I'm not searching for a dead body, I'm searching for my daughter, I believe she is alive."

"Me too, I believe my wife would be alive too, 'cos she's so strong. Where shall we go?"

"We probably should go to the hospital, wherever that is. Let's find out."

We drove out into the middle of the main street where there was a massive amount of traffic. We didn't even know where we were going, so we just followed the traffic.

We saw half a dozen bikies dressed in leather by the side of the road. I jumped out of the car and asked the boys if they knew where the Sanglah Hospital was. Three of them pointed up the street, they didn't speak English but they understood "Sanglah."

"Can you take us to the hospital or tell us how to get there?" I asked them.

"How much money have you got Craig?"

He said, "I dunno."

"Just give me all your money." I took all the money I had and gave it to one of the guys. I asked him to get on his bike and drive to the hospital and we would follow. He understood and jumped on his bike and we followed him to our destination.

When he pulled over, we were looking down on the hospital and it was like a movie set: there were big lights everywhere, masses of people running around and cars jammed everywhere. It was a nightmare. As we looked down on this horrific scene we told him we were looking for my daughter and Craig's wife. He looked up at us with a stunned look on his face and tossed our money back into Craig's hand. We thanked him and asked him how we could get down there. He pointed to a track and we ran down the hill to the hospital.

The Next Nightmare: Sanglah Hospital

It was a third-world hospital, with no bandages, no drugs, no needles, just nothing. We barged through and saw people screaming everywhere. More bodies were being brought in as we spoke, bodies from a garbage truck, bodies in cars, and there was a whole line of people outside with horrific injuries.

We went straight to the operating theater, for some reason it was the biggest room. It had four tables lined up with people being operated on by many Australian doctors with their holiday clothes on. There was no nurses or anesthetics, not even needles. They were operated on without anything, having bits and pieces cut off them and limbs removed with saws. The noise was incredible and what was also incredible was the lack of blood. I didn't realise this, but everybody's wounds had been cauterized in the fire—which is why there was no bleeding.

I found out what weak at the knees meant. I've heard that saying for years, when someone says, "I'm going weak at the knees," but I never really knew what it meant until that night. Craig pulled over a young lady to have a look if it was his wife. The woman had no face or distinguishing body features left. Craig started to fall over, and I caught him. He's a big guy so I went over with him. I said "Craig, come on. You can't do this now, get up!"

"What happened?" he questioned me.

"I think you went weak at the knees mate." I picked him up and slapped his face,

"I won't do that again."

"You can't. We've gotta find her."

We kept looking through all the bodies and the injured people on operating tables, and 5 minutes later there's Craig's face right in front of mine staring down at me.

I said, "What are you doing?"

"I caught you mate, you fell over."

I asked him if I went weak at the knees too, and he said yes you did! I had to pull myself up and slap myself around. We had to get back on the job of who we were looking for. I had the note the aunt wrote of everyone's names (which I still have to this day.) So we just kept searching and searching until there was nothing left to search.

When we came out the front door the sun was rising. It was almost daylight. I saw Tia at the front door and she started running towards me. I looked at her face and she looked at mine and we both knew—the question "is Chloe here?" didn't even need to be asked—the answer was no. I looked down, and she looked at me and said, "Look at your legs."

I thought about all the sharp stuff I saw at the bombsite and how the firemen's boots were cut to pieces, but I didn't think about my own feet or legs. They were black from the knees down with soot and whatever I had run through. I only had a pair of thongs on as I raced out the door with Tia to look for Chloe. I didn't think about what I was going to find or what I would be walking through. I suppose I should hose all this shit off, I thought. I had a sense my feet and legs are not going to be in real good shape. That's when I discovered that there's tough things in the world, like football players, tough fighters and boxers and everything like that, but nothing is tougher than the Australian thong. My legs and feet were completely undamaged— I didn't have a mark on me, not a scratch. My blue Australian thongs had done me well. Nothing is tougher than an Aussie thong.

We stayed in Bali over the next 5-6 days to keep searching for Chloe, with other parents flying over from Australia to help. We had a posse, it was a big gang and every day we would get up and go somewhere different to search. We searched different medical facilities and places where they were treating the injured because there were bodies all over Bali, people were taken to every medical facility in the region. During the search, there was no sign of Chloe—nor of Craig's wife.

We were going through another hospital again and we spotted a young guy we recognized from before who was crying. I asked him if he was ok, and he said, "My mum, I've lost my mum. She was on the dance floor and now I'm here and I can't find her." It was so tragic, I didn't know what to do to help him. He was beat up and badly burnt.

Later that day we were at another medical centre, about five kms away searching and asking around, when this lady stepped out and said, "Can you take me home?" We all looked up and it was Michelle, the young guy's mum. She was all burnt up and all us big tough macho guys standing there in our shorts and singlets were dumbstruck.

My wife Tia stepped forward and said, "Of course, we are taking you home, we are going now." We took her to the hospital first to her son, who she thought was dead. He thought she was dead too, so we reunited them and we got to see that moment of joy. That is what God does.

By now you may be wondering how God plays into this picture. If you believe in God, you've got to believe in the other bloke too, and this other bloke does a really good job. This wasn't God's work. It came from "the other bloke." But in times of strife, God helps. He puts people in your path, like the motorcycle guy with the kid. Experiences like that leaves a feeling that will never be forgotten. I can never remember a word anyone says, but I never forget how they make me feel. That's massive for me. I got a feeling from that I reckon. A feeling I still have today.

The day after the bombing, after only a couple of hours of sleep, I got up, stepped outside and looked across at the other apartments, where I saw my mate Dave on his verandah. He looked at me and me at him, and it was left unsaid. He knew what I knew and I knew what he knew: They were all dead. We walked towards each other crying and hugged. He said, "You know don't cha?" Dave is a fireman and he had seen a lot so he had a good grasp of the situation.

I said, "Of course I know."

And he said, "I know too. But we can't tell anyone."

We stayed for the rest of that week hoping to find Chloe, and then we went home to Sydney.

Back in Sydney

I'm still a parent and I have a flame that never goes out in the back of my head. Always a flame there. I always thought Chloe would come home. They were finding people kilometers away in houses and medical centres. They were finding people everywhere, so my little head was saying that could still happen to Chloe. I wasn't giving up even though I said those things to David. Despite everything, it wasn't going out—my flame wasn't going anywhere. I know she will be ok, I thought.

About two weeks after the bomb, there was knock at the front door. Oh crickey! I opened it and there was the lady from the Australian Federal Police who was liaising with us. She had this big smile on her face and my heart of course nearly jumped out of my chest. She said "Dave, Dave, we found her, we found Chloe, she is coming home tomorrow."

I could have kissed her. I said, "Oh darling thank you so much."

Then she realised what she did and how she said it. Her face changed and she said, "Oh I am so sorry, I think I said that wrong. She is coming home tomorrow in a coffin. We found the body and bits and pieces of her. I am so sorry Dave." Then she walked away and I closed the door.

I could see myself like it was an out of body experience, and I walked down the hall and washed the dishes. I still didn't believe her—that little flame just wouldn't go out. I didn't believe it. They have made a mistake. Dental records can be wrong, everything can be wrong. I'm a parent, I'm not giving up.

A counsellor we were working with named Julie heard the news and requested I go to see her. When I arrived she said, "I have to do this Dave, you are in denial."

I said "What do you mean denial?"

She said, "You're in denial about your daughter. I want to show you something." She put a photograph in front of me with a sheet of paper over it and said, "I know you've seen worse than this because people have told me what you did in Bali, but this is your girl." It was a photograph of Chloe and I thought it had to be one of the photographs of the kids on the dance floor pre-bombing with everyone having fun and plenty of laughter.

She said, "No Dave, this is Chloe in the morgue." She was so gentle and kind, and as she talked to me, she slowly lowered the paper on Chloe's last photograph.

There was her hair and her forehead, she had a beautiful forehead —but there was no face. A beam had fallen on her face and taken it away—and her jaw was hanging out while her brain was sticking out of the side of her head down to her neck, and there was a missing piece on the left side of her beautiful shoulders. She had beautiful arms, beautiful brown arms down to her elbows, but her arms were missing. They were laying beside her. Then she lowered the paper down to her beautiful legs. She had big thighs and lovely legs. She always had big feet and called them her ladies' eights. Chloe's legs down to her ladies' eights were missing— her legs were down to a point where her feet had been burnt off and that was the end of the photograph. That was my girl—that was my daughter. It was Chloe. That little flame that was always in the back of my mind was extinguished. It was the worst day of my life. Nothing comes close to that little flame being extinguished. Nothing. Everything I saw in the ruins of the nightclub, everything I saw in the hospital—nothing comes close to that flame going out and that loss of hope. She's gone just like that. The worst day of my life.

It was around the same time that Chloe's remains were identified that Craig was also given the news that his wife had perished in the bombings. Before her funeral in Sydney, Craig had the courage to open the coffin to view her body. Amongst her charred remains, there was a little hair left on her head, He cut off two small tuffs of hair to save for his two daughters, and put it in two lockets for them to wear.

Take one day at a time, just a day at a time.

I had counselling with a few people including Julie Dunstall (the woman who showed me the photo.) She is a lovely counsellor. We talked about a lot of things, including many of the things we discussed here. It took me a few years, but I had to stop the misery. I couldn't go on living the way I was living after that day in Julie's office. Life was so dark and I was dragging my feet every day. It had to STOP!

If you're going to get on with life, you gotta make a decision. I can't walk around all day kicking my jaw with a long face, and no one will blame me if I did. But that's not Chloe. She would hate to see me do that.

So instead I think of a lot of good things, fun things we did together, and I step forward, step up, and enjoy this life.

There's a lot of people that go through a lot more than what I've been through, a lot of people. I can't disgrace them by being sad. I've gotta get on with life because this isn't a dress rehearsal, this is the main game. I just have to step up to the main game and do the best I can on a daily basis. The next right thing, that's all I have do. The next right thing because that is always followed by the next right thing after that—and it works.

Life is not fair in a lot of ways, but it is still good. It is still really good. I can see my daughter's laughter in a lot of people. I can see so much of her everywhere I look. I can see her in the corner of my eyes sometimes. I can see her slicking her hair and she is laughing. I can see it when I see my mum and dad too. I often hear my mum saying bastard. That was my name when I was a kid—"the bastard"—because mum is from Tasmania so of course I did some bastardly things—I was a cheeky bugger.

I live life to its fullest as much as I can, with as many good thoughts as I can. Every morning when I wake up my first thought is always of my daughter, which is closely followed by the bombing and all that went on in that horrible period of time. It goes through my mind in just one nanosecond! The next conscious thought is Chloe's laughter, and how big her laugh was. It is so infectious—it infected everybody who was with her—whenever she started laughing everybody laughed. She laughed a lot. Everyone loved her laughter. She found humour in everything. If you stubbed your toe she'd laugh her head off. When I think of that, my day starts off right. She had the best spirit. I am sure she is still laughing.

The grief side of it . . . I still get that pretty regularly. There's a lot of triggers in this life. Grief doesn't leave you, it just hides and comes back in another shape. I can see something on the television on the news or another terrorist attack and what that does is it puts me back to the bombsite. Straight back to the hospital. That's where I go when I see awful things that trigger me. Then I have to say not today—not now. I do that a lot but that's OK because that's my life. Other people have their life and that's my life. I'm not going to hurt anybody else. It's very important not to dump your negative stuff on people. I can turn a negative thought away by thinking of Chloe riding a wave, and it helps me stay positive. Wallowing is not good, and I want life to be good.

Girl with the Frangipanis in Her Hair

I was surfing at Bondi one day, not too long after Bali, and I thought wouldn't it be nice if I could get a little painting of Chloe on the wall near the third ramp where I always park my car and where all the longboarders surf? I called the council and they gave me this chap's phone number. His name was Steve Ziergo, otherwise known by Droogie, his nickname. He was the artist at the Ways Youth Centre.

I gave him a ring and said, "How do you do? My name is Dave."

"I know who you are, you're Chloe's dad. I had a dream and in this dream I was asked to paint a portrait of Chloe—I've got this! It has to be big."

All I fucking said was hello. I said, "Start again mate!"

He said, "I had a dream about this, I dreamt about this phone call."

"You are kidding me."

"No." he siad.

We went down to the beach to the wall next to the third ramp, he said "I've got this spot up here, it is two slabs of wall—they are mine. The council gave it to me to paint and I'm going to do something really nice for you."

And he did. He put up this lovely mural and it's been there for over 15 years now. It's the most photographed part of the wall on the beach. It is Chloe's face with frangipani flowers around her, and there are the names of the Australians killed in the Bali bombings that year, including the 6 footballers from the Coogee dolphins. There are also 18 doves, which signifies the 18 people from this state who passed away.

Laurie Wilson, the local tourist guy from the council who knows Chloe's story, takes groups of tourists to see it every day. He explains the story behind the mural and they all take photos and all love it. It's really nice.

One day after an almighty storm, most of the sand from Bondi Beach ended up on the promenade. The promenade was completely covered in 6ft of sand, it looked like there was no sand left on the beach. They had to get the sand off the cars and the walk way where all the murals were, to get it back into the ocean and onto the beach. The whole promenade was buried in sand—except for Chloe's painting. There was a big ditch and her painting was untouched. I remember someone took a photo and sent it to me and said, "Look Dave, even God wouldn't dare cover her up!"

Marday

During the days we spent looking for Chloe after the bomb, we employed one of the young boys we knew, Marday, as our driver. A lovely kid. In 2002 he was only 18. He worked so hard for us. He didn't stop looking for Chloe for days and days on his motorcycle. He hardly slept, he just loved Chloe and wanted to find her alive as much as we did.

Cut a long story short, we didn't go back to Bali for 10 years, we just couldn't go, the thought of being back there was too hard. But finally we went back because our son Jarad bribed us. He said he was going to Bali with his wife and two children for a holiday. We were shocked and told him he couldn't go—he couldn't take our grandkids to such a place. He told us that we weren't listening to him—and he was going to take his family to Bali. Further, he said that if we wanted to come we were welcome, otherwise we could just stay home.

My wife and I wondered what we were going to do. Tia said we had to go to protect the kids. So that was our call to go back to Bali. Tia's fears came flooding back when we landed. She was really jittery as we sat in the plane waiting to embark. She said to me, "I don't think I can do this. Why are we here?"

"For the grandchildren, of course," I said.

When we landed the smell was the same, which brought back lots of memories, but nothing else was the same, we recognized nothing—except for Marday's big beaming smile. He had come to meet us, and it was so lovely to see him again. After many hugs and tears we jumped into his van. On the back of his van was a "for sale" sign.

"I sold my van yesterday, Mr. David."

"Are you going to upgrade?"

"No, Mr David, I can't pay the bill. I can't pay the bank anymore. So I had to sell it."

I looked at my wife. She said, "Whatever you do, I will support you 100%."

The next day I asked Marday to take us to his bank. To cut a long story short, I paid off his van and his motorcycle in one loan. Marday, now married, was standing outside the bank with his wife and two little kiddies. He gave me the registration forms of the vehicles because he thought I now owned them and he worked for me.

"No, Marday, these are yours. It is all yours."

"No, Mr. David, you pay these, now they are yours."

"This is our gift to you and your family, Marday."

He explained this to his wife in Indonesian and she started to cry. Then the kids started crying. He's crying, she's crying, Tia's crying, but not me, I'm a man, I don't cry!

(Ok, ok I did, I cried.)

We got to do foreign aid and cut out the middle man. We changed the life of a family for just a few thousand dollars. That felt the best, it was the next right thing to do.

We go back to Bali now every year, and we do the next right thing every year: We employ Marday to look after us. We pay him way more than he should get paid, we like to do it, and we always look after his wife and kids.

Yes, I must note that we now enjoy going back to Bali. There has been healing and our family can once again enjoy a place in the world we have always loved to visit. By putting light on what's happened, it has no power over me. That's very important for me. The memories can be draining and tiring, but I shine that light on it so it doesn't hide in the dark places of my mind. I have to say I am proud of myself, through all of this, I never picked up a drink or a drug to help me through the pain. I sometimes lose my temper, but I can put that away.

Life's good. It's not fair, but it's still bloody good!

God's Pillow

Going through this tragedy, and seeing everything I saw in the hours and days after the bombings, has made me much more compassionate. I've also developed what I call God's pillow. That's the two or three seconds I take to respond to something that's happening I don't like. I don't react anymore, I respond and lean on God's pillow. If someone beeps a horn from a car and they yell "you idiot" or something like that—I take that 2 or 3 seconds and think, it could be someone rushing to the hospital with a sick child. It could be any number of things they need help or a hand with, and by the time I've said that to myself there's no anger left. There's no reaction, I get to respond instead via God's pillow. Thank you god.

I now really enjoy my beautiful granddaughters, just like I used to play with Chloe. They smile at me sometimes and it is so similar to Chloe's smile. Even though they are white as snow and Chloe was a little brown beach babe (my little Wahini girl) Lulu's laugh and affection is the same in many ways.

I also discovered how important it is to keep your sense of humour.

I was asked to speak for the first anniversary of the bombing, to represent all the families involved, and I was so honoured. The anniversary is held at Dolphin Point in Coogee every year on the date of the bombing. The Premier was talking and it was packed.

I was working with God's gift, a woman named Diane Brian, who is the lady who looks after everything and everyone during the event. Before the presentation she looked at me and said, "Now listen Dave . . . ." She appeared nervous.

"What?" I asked.

"There are a lot of people here and TV cameras, if you get lost or concerned, just look at me. I'll stand near you, so just take everyone else out of focus and look at me."

"That's good darling, where will you be standing? And where is the power box for all the microphones?

"They're over there near the container. Why?"

"Could you stick near that? You might need to hit the off switch."

"You can't turn the power off—everything will go out."

"Unfortunately, I should have mentioned this before, I have Tourette's syndrome. If I suddenly start swearing and cursing, you are going to have to turn the switch off immediately."

She nearly fell over with a heart attack! She had put so much work into this day She started to wobble. When I said it, I could see what was going through her mind—I could see her imagining me blurting out all these swear words. I had to catch her and apologise.

"I'm sorry darl'."

"How could you think of that?"

"I don't know, but it made me laugh and it made you laugh."

She never let me forget my prank. You've gotta laugh, you have to have fun. I want to make my day positive every day, because life is too short to keep wallowing in all of the negativity. This decision I make every morning to focus on the good is the difference between a good life and a bad one.

About Dave Byron

Dave Byron lives with his wife in Sydney Australia. He enjoys his granddaughters and loves to take them surfing at Bondi beach as much as he can.

I Died to Learn How to Live

Krista Gorman

While I've either spoken or written about my story multiple times, it never fails to move me to tears. The intensity of the experience, the energy it held, is reborn each time I recount the different stages of it. I am always transported back, once again watching my dead body below as I transitioned into a loose cloud of thousands of vibrating particles before being swept away on the journey of a lifetime.

I had married and become pregnant during my two years of training to be a Physician's Assistant, and was due to give birth only three weeks after my graduation. Because of a medical issue detected early on in my pregnancy, I was to be induced into labor a week before my due date. On the morning of July 17, 2000, I'd been in my hospital room for thirteen hours, and my contractions were still not regular. I hadn't dilated very much, and our baby started showing signs of distress.

I'd already had an epidural administered, and as my midwife placed an internal monitor into my baby's scalp to better keep track of her vital signs, I began having trouble breathing. Rapidly, this trouble turned into gasping for air. No matter how hard I tried, I couldn't get enough, and as I made my last desperate attempt to draw air into my lungs, a divine

74

peace suddenly came over me. There in the hallway as I was rushed into the operating room, I let go. My heart stopped at 9:18.

My next moment of awareness was of watching thousands of tiny black particles racing up from what I now know was my body lying on a bed below. They collected in a loose, static like cloud around where my vision was and sort of hung there, gently moving in the air much like a buoy floating in the ocean.

I was utterly and completely in awe! Still "Krista" with only the sense of sight remaining, I was still the "me" I am now; but in a pure, unattached form. There was no time, no past or future, only that instant. I had no thoughts about anything, only feeling, and I felt completely and utterly free! Unencumbered by my physical body, I was timeless and eternal and felt absolutely amazing! It was as if the physical body had never existed and all that did exist was my consciousness.

Looking around, I was so far above my body yet close to it at the same time. The scene unfolding below was completely unrecognizable. I had no understanding of what any of it was. The wall to my left had taken on a fluid-like quality, and I noticed the line of wallpaper across the top. Looking down, I felt curious about what was going on below and wanted to know more. I saw my doctor take something from my stomach and hand it to a person at my right shoulder, who took the bundle in a blue drape and turned their back to me. I wanted to know what was in her arms and increasingly felt more of a desire to learn about what was happening down below. I then saw someone in blue step into the doorway, and after surveying the situation briefly, watched him step up to the bedside. I now know that it was another doctor who arrived to help my obstetrician deliver my baby by emergency C-section, along with a cardiologist and a cardiothoracic surgeon who, thankfully, happened to be there that morning.

Back in the room, I felt myself becoming more and more attached to what was happening below. It started to feel so familiar, and I could almost recognize what it was but couldn't quite get it, much like that tip-of-the-tongue phenomenon where you know the word, it's right there, but you just can't remember it!

With the growth in my desire to know and my greater attachment to the scene unfolding below, I then felt a sort of tug to my left. Something was pulling at me as if to say "Come on." I resisted, as I wanted to continue watching what was happening below and find out more about it. Persistently, it tugged with more force. At that point, I knew I was to go where it wanted me to go, and my resistance turned to acceptance. In the instant that shift happened, off I went!

Moving at the speed of light I was whisked out of the room, through a flash of bright white space and into a dense, dark one. It was made up of the same particulate matter as me and I merged with it, into it, and was blissfully reabsorbed. It felt like coming home, like I was where I'd always been and would always be. I was reconnected again with my source, and the connection was utterly indescribable! It was a deep, eternal, everlasting love that was absolutely everything.

As I sped along, I could still see and feel but no other senses were present. I had no thinking mind, no body, just space. I was one with the darkness that also held specks of light. There were liquid grey-white-black spots alongside me that would become dense and particulate again in the next instant.

Then, suddenly I slowed and felt a rushing of information, a sort of download. In an instant I'd received the answers to all the questions I'd ever had in my life, like they were all being asked, one right after the other, and answered, with others being asked on top of those and others on top of those, all simultaneously, and the answer boiled down to one word. Love. The answer to absolutely everything was Love.

The feeling I had was of pure amazement and gratitude and understanding. I felt like I'd known that on some level, but was now shown it. It was now confirmed for me as truth. I'd been gifted the actual experience of it. Words don't come close to describing how that felt. Not even close.

To my left, off in the distance, was a tiny white speck. I was drawn to it and as I began moving toward it, the speck grew until it was a large grey-white circular opening. I could see figures in the opening, shadowy human-like figures were there, and one figure, in particular, needed my help. In front of all the others was a little boy. I felt he was about seven years old and reminded me of a little Tom Sawyer; with a wide-brimmed hat and overalls. The feeling I felt from him was not of fear or anything "bad," merely that he wanted help.

As I floated into the space, the adult shadow beings that had been huddled behind him fanned out in a line, and as I drifted deeper into the space, passing them as I did, I realized the boy was gone. I was now surrounded by the adult beings that all needed my help. I could feel their need and wanted to help each of them. Sensing my desire to give of myself, they began to come at me one by one, and then dart away. One at a time in succession they'd come at me, steal one of my particles, and then depart. Over and over this continued until I could feel myself dwindling, slowly fading away much the same as I had in the hallway before my heart stopped beating.

My next feeling was the realization of what was happening. I didn't want to lose myself in there, I wanted to survive and immediately felt a desire to leave. No sooner from when the feeling came into being that I was moving again, out of that space and back into the dense particulate matter. This time it was only a brief stay, as I found myself moving through another opening that emerged into what I call my Eden.

It was a brilliant, gorgeous, simply breathtaking landscape of yellow flowers spanning the ground in front of me met by deep green rolling hills dotted with trees off in the distance. To my left was a crystal clear, sparkling waterfall with moss covered rocks. To my right, a dense evergreen forest.

I felt myself, my energy, immediately merge with it. The sweet, gentle beauty of the flowers and I were one. The glorious blue sky and trees and grass were my very essence, and the rocky waterfall and forest flowed in and through me and I with them. We were a seamless flow of love energy, creational energy. It was completely blissfully incredible, the pure, divine love that was everything. Every particle of me and every particle of the landscape vibrated to the same frequency of that divine love. It was ecstasy!

In the midst of that, two very tall, thin, beige beings flanked me on either side. They were benevolent guides, my angels, and ready to support me. They were the embodiment of unconditional love and immeasurable strength and gave me three choices: I could stay there in what I call my Eden, I could move on to what came next, or I could return to my life.

I had no understanding of any of my choices, other than that of my Eden, yet staying there did not feel like the "right" choice. Going beyond it didn't either. Not knowing why, I chose to return to my life, although I didn't remember nor had any understanding—I just knew that was what I was supposed to do at that point. It was as if I had some higher knowing of what coming back here would entail, but not fully aware of what it was within that present state of consciousness; like it was withheld on purpose so as to allow for the creational aspect of my 3D experience to happen without already knowing the outcome. I still had some work to do.

Once my choice to return was made, I started racing backward away from my Eden and my guides. I watched as they turned slightly toward me and communicated that if I was going to come back, I needed to share what I learned there.

Without any hesitation, I agreed.

My next memory was of feeling a terrible pain in my chest. I was back in my body. It was 9:26 a.m.

What I later learned was that I'd suffered an amniotic fluid embolism or AFE followed by disseminated intravascular coagulation, or DIC, and spent two days in the ICU before being moved to a room, and then discharged from the hospital one week after my daughter was born. Maggie was born with a pulse of sixty beats per minute, and that's all. She was not moving. She was not breathing. She was blue. After reviving her, she was quickly transferred to a neonatal intensive care unit at a nearby hospital. We wouldn't meet for the first time until she was five days old. I was discharged one week after my daughter's birth and my death.

For several weeks after coming home from the hospital, I was in another world. I'd carried the energy of the afterlife with me: that divine love was still there, within me, flowing through me, as I almost robotically went about my daily activities. Initially, I couldn't remember details about anything regarding my previous life and my family had to watch me very closely. At that point I had no recall of my NDE, yet was behaving completely differently than I had before.

Prior to my death, I was a type A-personality. I was organized and somewhat regimented. Afterward, I literally had no cares in the world. The anxiety I always felt about nearly everything was completely gone, my intensity had dissolved into a pure acceptance and peace, and they really didn't know what to make of me! I loved everything and everyone and knew that all was well in life. In fact, I believed everyone felt the same way I did! I had no idea that the people around me didn't feel just as loving and loved as me, just as accepting of everyone and everything as I was, and peaceful beyond measure.

My family simply didn't know what to make of me. The thing was, I'd been fundamentally changed, to the very level of my DNA. I was pieced back together in a completely different way, and with a new knowledge and experience of the divine love that is the "who" and "what" we are. It was everything! I had no explanation for the change, nor did I even realize I'd changed at all. At that point, I still hadn't remembered my experience in the afterlife.

In the weeks that followed, every few days I'd wake up and feel more like the "old Krista." I'd have more of my memory back and found myself reconnecting more and more with my life here. Things around me were becoming more familiar and as that happened, I was also becoming more and more attached to the 3D world.

Then, one beautiful morning I awoke after having a dream. It was a dream so vivid, so real. In fact, it was hyper-real, surpassing any known experience of what we call "reality" here. In my dream state, I'd re-experienced my NDE.

I laid there completely amazed . . . I was literally ecstatic with joy and totally overwhelmed with love and appreciation, confusion and elation. I shouted for my then husband who came running into the bedroom with an anxious, confused look on his face. Then, sitting there in bed, with tears of joy and amazement and pure awe running down my face, I recounted my experience as he listened intently. When I'd finished telling him what I'd learned he gave me a big hug and words of support, which were perfect, yet I felt so let down. He didn't really understand. He was just grateful I was alive, while there I was, having just had the memory of my NDE given to me. It was as if I'd only just experienced it, with no one to share it with who could really understand. I felt let down and disappointed, overwhelmed and elated all at the same time.

While I needed support, so did those around me. My ex-husband was a touring musician, and in the middle of making an album, so though he wanted to be there more, he wasn't able to. My baby needed her mother and the dishes done and the laundry folded. My full presence in my life was required, which left little time for my healing body and brain to process what I'd been through. In my attempt to cope with the enormity of my experience and all I had to cope with, my ego crept in and I began to doubt what I had recalled and tried to convince myself it was just a dream. However, my higher self knew better; through my higher self I knew it wasn't a dream! The battle would ultimately go on for months until I made the decision to believe that my NDE was meant only for me; that way I wouldn't have to make the changes it required for me to live in this world as the love I am.

I didn't know how to "be" the blissful I felt in the afterlife. I would have to learn how to do it, but knew it would require drastic external changes in my life, changes that felt far too overwhelming with all I had going on at the time. Holding my NDE and its message close allowed me to stay locked inside my ego-self and protected me from being hurt by the outside world, that world that I loved and, as long as my ego was present, still also feared.

During that time I decided to do some research on Near Death Experiences and the medical community. At that point, my ego was flaring up and I wanted to hold back on sharing my experience with others while at the same time wanting answers to my questions about it. I ultimately decided to email a physician named Jeffery Long who studied the NDE phenomena. I thought, as a doctor I could trust his opinion. Such ego! In my email I made sure to sound vague and did not mention I'd recalled my NDE in a dream, and instead said I thought maybe something had happened during the eight minutes I was without a heartbeat.

It was his response that completely knocked me off my ego pedestal. "Pay attention to your dreams." I burst into tears. Someone who was a scientist like me and knew what I'd been through understood and had just validated me.

In the years that followed I continued my daily struggle with life on life's terms all the while wanting something else. My NDE remained a fixture in the back of my mind as I searched outside of myself for satisfaction in my life. Happiness always felt out of reach, and despite the fact that I'd experienced such undefinable divine love, I always felt unworthy of it. I tried to distract myself from myself through focusing on my daughter, on work, projects, etc. Nothing really brought me joy except being with my little girl. She was my angel and in my darkest hours, my guiding light.

My struggle with finding happiness and contentment in my life persisted for many years after my NDE. Looking back, what I've come to understand is that this period was a training ground for me. It was the time I needed to experience what I experienced so I could serve in the way I came back to serve. I was learning how to live in this world the tough way, the harder way, by resisting my true self from coming forth into the world so I could experience the opposite of what I actually came back to do and help others do, too. I had to learn how to love myself in this body form and then practice that self-love on a daily basis.

In the many years since my NDE, I've traveled a journey of self-rediscovery and reintegration in this life, one which has entailed too many challenges and triumphs to recount, but suffice to say each and every one has led me to the amazing place I am at now. I am eternally grateful for all of the challenges.

I've traveled a path of learning to live in this world again with the knowledge and experience of actually experiencing the divine love that not only I am but the love we all are, because the "I" that I am is the same "I" that you are. We are true reflections of one another and divine representations of a benevolent, ultimate energy that we call the Universe. Everything is this love energy; we are absolutely seamless with it. The hydrogen and oxygen that makes up a single water molecule in the vast ocean are the same elements that make up a water molecule within our bodies. Plants and trees that thrive on the hydrogen dioxide we expire produce the oxygen we take in. These are but two examples amongst thousands that support our interconnectedness with all that is.

The gift of having the experience of what it feels like to actually feel that seamlessness was one of the fundamental things that helped me reconnect to myself in the years after my reintegration into the world. It took a long time for me to do that and a big reason for the time it took was ego. I was fearful of losing all I had around me. I had changed so deeply, so fundamentally that it was simply too much for me to handle. I then buried my experience because acknowledging it created too much pain. I struggled day after day to understand how I was to fulfill my promise to share what I'd learned in the afterlife, while at the same time being resistant to it. I was already a "good" person, I thought. Therefore, how much more of a good person was I supposed to be? Love was what it was all about, so then what?

The piece I was missing was that it wasn't just love that it was all about. The lesson I'd learned in the afterlife had shown me something much more fundamental. It had taught me self-love. Loving ourselves is the single most important thing we could do on this earth because from that perspective flows all other forms of divine love.

For many years following my NDE I struggled daily with self-love. I continually denied my self the gift of experiencing that beautiful grace that comes with truly loving ourselves at any given moment. It wasn't anyone's fault; no one prevented me from caring for myself. What prevented me was ego. My beautiful ego used its influence to place energetic barriers to re-experiencing my higher self in this form, and the more I can intend love in any given moment, the less influence ego has in that same moment. To help myself live as my "true" self, the love I am, I created Twelve Principles for Daily Living. These principles ultimately helped me heal in a very deep, fundamental way, helping to bring forth my divine loving light to shine in this world. They guide me in my daily life so I may stay connected to the eternal divine love and light that I am and help me live a 5D existence in this 3D world.

These Principles, along with the Law of Attraction and meditation, saved my life and helped heal my family at a time of significant struggle and discord. They are what helped bring me into the beautiful new life I'm living today.

Because of my NDE, because of all the pain and struggle through the years following it, I was brought to a place in my life where I was ready to begin to really live as the person I knew myself to be, the person I'd experienced in the afterlife. I was ready to be that message of love so I could share it with the world.

In 2014 I wrote a book about my NDE and outlined the Twelve Principles for Daily Living. I decided to call it *I Died And Learned How To Live* and chose a painting my daughter had done for its cover. I remember seeing it for the first time, coming across it in her room and its energy affected me so powerfully. It's of a red heart lying on its side with a rainbow of color emanating from it. It felt broken and hopeful, beautiful and pure, and a perfect representation of all of us.

That book brought me to some amazing places. The greatest of which are the connections with other beautiful souls that I've been so incredibly fortunate to make along my life's path. Life is about relationships, it's about seeing us reflected in the other and responding with love. Through that we discover who we are and get to go deeper into the experience of being that person here on this earth.

The Twelve Principles for Daily Living are:

1. Live in Awareness

Each one of us is a divine manifestation of the divine universe, which is pure conscious love, and we're all connected by it. We are the creators of our experiences here and in the afterlife, along with the benevolent universe. We have the ability, through the Law of Attraction, to manifest anything we desire and to change our circumstances with a change in our "mind"; thus changing our vibration. The energetic resources of the universe are at our disposal and each of us is a touch point for those forces to be inflected in whichever direction we choose by using our free will and intention.

2. Live Willingly

To live willingly is to remain ever a student, open and ready to learn the lessons inherent in everything that occurs. Our lives don't happen to us, they happen through us, fueled by the benevolent energy of the universe and filtered through our physical form in a constant, never-ending flow.

In order to maintain that flow, we must decrease our resistance to it. When we are resisting "what is" – we create stress. Stress only brings about suffering and we must let go of suffering to let in joy. That process involves opening up our mind and heart to accepting all of life's experiences as they occur without exception and without judgment, knowing they are there to help us move further along our life's path.

3. Live Lovingly

To live from love is to nurture our connection to the love energy we are all touch points for on this earth. Through nurturing our connection we allow for the energy to flow through us, and outward to all those around us. Our beliefs about whom and what we are directly reflect the strength of our conscious connection; and when they are in alignment with love, it is a strong one. Our thoughts and deeds are filtered through it and reflected in our relationships. When we intend the highest and brightest feeling for ourselves, we can then share the whole of who and what we are with others. We are love; it's what makes up every cell in our bodies. Once we get in touch with that and are able to digest and manifest it in our lives through what we think, what we say and how we act, our lives can't help but improve.

4. Live Fearlessly

Fear is such a powerful factor in our lives and can lead us down a path of literal self-destruction. The human tendency is to live from a fear-based perspective; it's where our thoughts, choices and actions originate. In our essential nature, we're meant to expand and thrive, yet fear constricts and keeps us locked inside.

Fear is the opposite of love and the equivalent of ego. While they are both equally important for us to embrace, when ego dominates our consciousness there is no room for love. For many of us, ego is the stronger of the two and overshadows our awareness of the love we are; and hinders our ability to connect with others in a meaningful way.

While the experience of ego is just as essential as the experience of love and is the provider of contrast in this world, it is also the source of our suffering.

5. Live Compassionately

When we're able to identify with another's suffering, we can then act to alleviate it. A feeling or act of compassion is the physical manifestation of the recognition of our self in the other; it is a mirror of the divinity inherent in every one of us. What distinguishes the recognition of that divinity is the level of conscious understanding of our own.

Embedded within the feeling of compassion is the feeling of love. The experience of true compassion is an essential part of why we're together on this earth and exemplifies the fact that we are all intimately interconnected.

6. Live Patiently

Patience is a side effect of living fearlessly. When we are living without fear, we're able to be in the moment, free from the need to control outcomes. Patience allows for us to really experience the moment, to be present and open to whatever happens within it. What freedom! When we're present and open there is an opportunity to exercise our free will through the filter of awareness of who and what we are, then use our intention to create the next moment.

7. Live Presently

When we're able to bring our full awareness into what's happening right now, we give all of our energy to it and anything is possible. Through our thoughts, intention and free will we are able to influence the energy of the moment in whichever direction we desire, thus creating our lives. Anything and everything is possible.

8. Live Spiritually

This involves the practice of living our lives with an understanding of our divine nature and the divine nature of everyone and everything. We are spiritual beings manifest in the physical body, and the physical body is not the be all and end all of our existence. It is finite, infinite and ever changing; therefore spirituality is wherever we are in our present state of awareness and is always in flux.

9. Live Faithfully

Living faithfully is to believe in our ability to bring forth our true nature and live from that truth until we experience the joy and ecstasy of life. Faith lies in the awareness that what we see is not the end of the road. There is more to it, much more than what we perceive with the five senses; and until we experience that, we must have faith in its presence.

Faith encompasses trust and belief in the natural unfolding of life to its greatest good. It allows for a life of greater ease and comfort and for the other Principles to manifest.

10. Live Purposefully

We must commit each day to bringing forth the love that we are and direct our energy toward the things that help us do it. We're here to create the life we desire to live. There is purpose in all that we do, from the mundane to the miraculous and everything, all of it, is a necessary part of that creation.

11. Live Creatively

We are creative beings, and bring our creative energy into everything we do. Through that creativity, we manifest the divine energy of the universe that is the same divine energy we all share. When we allow that energy to manifest in its purest form and feel how it's guiding us, we can then express it in a way that brings us happiness and joy. Each of us is a touch point for the energetic resources of the universe and we join forces with it in the creation of our lives.

12. Live Miraculously

Miracles occur everywhere, all the time and we are both the creators and co-creators of them. It's through our desires and intentions that we make miracles in our lives and when we're able to recognize and stand in awe of the life we've created, we stand in the natural flow of the universe and get to experience a life lived to the highest of possibilities.

Every one of us has the potential for living a miraculous life, one in accordance with who we are in our deepest state of being, and is a reflection of heaven on earth.

There have been some major changes in my life since my NDE, changes that have profoundly changed my life and the lives of those around me. One of which was the divorce of my husband and I. That part of our individual and collective journey ended to bring about the beginning of a new one, one that has brought such incredible expansion – so much more love and joy into my life! I've met my Twin Soul, my other half, in Ainsley, who also had a NDE. Together we are walking a path of love and light to share with the world. I never knew I could be loved so deeply, so purely, and love equally in return. Allowing for that love to permeate and integrate into our being required for ego to take a back seat. Had we both resisted and continued to do so, our relationship would not have been able to develop in the divine way it has.

This kind of higher love is possible for everyone if we can release ourselves from the confines of ego and open up to the all-encompassing beauty of Love.

I love you all!

About Krista Gorman, PA-C

Krista Gorman is a Physician Assistant and Author who, only three weeks after graduating from her PA training program, suffered cardiopulmonary arrest and died while in labor with her daughter.

In the wake of her NDE she created the *Twelve Principles For Daily Living* that helped heal her life through reconnecting her to the divine love energy we are. It is her life's purpose to lovingly help others on their personal journeys through using what she learned in the afterlife.

Krista works as a Physician Assistant in Emergency Medicine, holds a Bachelor of Science degree in psychology and, as all parents are, is the mother of a divine miracle.

A Lifetime of Evidence

Frances Ray Key

I snuggled down in my bed, a peaceful smile on my lips. I had just spent time with my mother assembling some of my poetry into a notebook. When my mother had written the title of the book on the front: "Thoughts are Things", adding a triangle and a square as a cover design, my heart had swelled with an unnamable sense of fulfillment. The written word had always been my first love, starting at age three when I picked up a first-grade book and read it fluently. Now, I had created my own book, a set of poems about light, love and magic. My mother had let me stay up an hour past my nine-year-old bedtime to finish it! Best of all, there was someone who loved what I wrote and couldn't wait to read it - my beloved mother.

As I rested in this state of happiness, I was astonished to see a mist in the shape of a woman's dress forming in front of her bed. The skirt started at the floor and revealed itself bit by bit. Gradually, the skirt, the waist, the chest, the arms, the face and hair materialized. Along with the beautiful vision came a feeling of elation and ecstasy, new yet somehow familiar. All of a sudden, my mother re-entered the room and the misty lady vanished. "Mother!" I cried out, "I've been uplifted!"

Breathlessly, I described the event to her, she was happy as she was able to explain to me what the apparition was. A spiritual guide or angel, and she explain why I had attracted her through my spiritual writing, which was part of my life's destiny. We talked into the night about the world of the soul, the Other Side, our life's purpose, and how I had been so connected to the unseen realms since I was very little. She described to me how we come to the Earth to work as a group on certain projects. Some of our group stay on the Other Side and some of us are here together. It was a concept she would often repeat throughout her life - and beyond her death.

I have never forgotten this experience. It was the first of its kind in my life, and the start of my soul's conscious connection to the Other Side, a connection encouraged and guided by my mother. She was my spiritual guide, teacher, and friend - a role that remained steady throughout my life and has continued beyond her transition in 2010. She created a childhood for me that nurtured my spiritual leanings, my writing ability, my musical talents, and my longing to be of service in the world. As the course of my life unfolded, with many emotional ups and downs, my mother was by my side, witnessing the many times I had mystical experiences such as the one I'd had in childhood. These experiences included the appearances of apparitions, an ability to do automatic writing, premonitory dreams and visions, and a continuous stream of spiritual poetry that sounded somewhat archaic in nature.

My mother helped me navigate it all. She understood because she had left an intensely Catholic background to seek a broader perspective when I turned five years old. Looking back, I understand now that she was led in that direction so she would be prepared to understand her unusual daughter. I cannot imagine what would have become of me as a child had I not had someone who comprehended the experiences I had.

The years rolled by, and being the pioneering spirit that she was, Mother explored life in a remarkable way. She forged into uncharted territory by opening a daycare and private school in 1953 in a time when most women were still living the "housewife" lifestyle. She was a loving and tough teacher, making her revered and respected. Parents and children alike marveled at her ability to tame the wildest child and do so with a smile on her beautiful face and a sparkle in her bright green eyes. She supplied a heavenly life for my sister and me, as we lived in a house attached to the daycare and school. We had a hundred children to play with anytime we wanted to walk out our kitchen door. Throughout the years, she would be approached by many adults who would say, "Are you Mrs. Key? I went to your school and those were the happiest days of my life."

Her first-grade classroom was also where I learned to read, playing around at her feet at the age of three. One day, I walked up to her and said, "I can read that book," and did so. It was to shape the foundation of my life, and true to form, it came through my mother. In the same way, my love of classical music was established. Mother had a gorgeous, warm contralto voice that had been professionally trained in Australia. She continued voice lessons in the USA and would take me with her. I would sit under the grand piano and listen to her vocalize and master many sacred and secular classical pieces.

Mother searched for Truth in many avenues, and took me along with her to explore various churches and groups. She always emphasized service to the world, humility and kindness. She saw a common thread of these themes throughout all religions. One day, someone introduced her to the works of Stewart Edward White and the lights came on for her. She said "I felt like I could have written the book. It was pure Truth to me, and I carried the book around with me for months, remaining in a state of bliss." About that time, she began attending an evening group at a Unitarian Church. I was ten, and she took me along. They were discussing automatic writing, and she wanted to share my poetry with them. I'd told Mother that "someone helps me" when I wrote, and the contact had even given me his name. One thing led to another, and soon I was doing automatic writing for the group with a blindfold on, answering questions they would ask. My abilities progressed rapidly, but when I entered my teens, I began to withdraw from them. I believe my teenage angst simply caused too much conflict for me at the time, and I needed to experience more concrete "earth life."

After she closed her school at about age 60, Mother became a Shelter Mother at a runaway home for teenagers. She lived in that center part-time and deeply loved the work. Eventually, she opened her own state-approved shelter home for sexually abused girls. At age 65 she received the "Shelter Mother of the Year" award for our city. Nobody who knew her was surprised. Her world consisted of outreach to others, primarily children, as she faithfully "walked her talk." As the years went by, she would tell me, "You should do that automatic writing you did as a child," and I would tell her, "You should write a book about the spiritual wisdom you've gained in your life." Neither of us pursued these things at the time, but we would certainly do so at a later date.

When Mother was diagnosed with lung cancer in 2008 at the age of 84, we were shocked. She was the same dynamo she had ever been and had shown so little sign of illness. The cancer was advanced, but she knocked it into remission through treatment for about five months. When it returned, I stayed home with her and took care of her. While I was filled with constant fear and great anticipatory grief of her passing, I was nonetheless deeply aware of the sacredness of our time together. Those twenty months with her were a tremendous gift, and while the family all wanted more, we were so fortunate to have even that much time.

Hospice helped us to keep Mother home so my sister, her boyfriend, one of my daughters and myself were able to be with her the night she passed. At the moment of her transition, I was filled with a strange sensation which I did not understand until much later. It was as if a piece of my being went with her to the Other Side, and a piece of her entered my form and stayed here. Clearly, it was this exchange of our "spiritual DNA" that enabled the remarkable events that followed.

Determined to be a source of strength to everyone else and to give her some kind of formal acknowledgment of her tremendous service to the world, I read a prayer over Mother's body that I had written a few months before. I felt unusually calm. In the ensuing days after, this feeling of strength persisted even though I was awash with deep grief and loss. I knew I'd been forever changed. Some part of me was no longer present - the part of me that had so often been angry and frustrated in my life. I described it to someone as if "All the Frankie-ness is gone." And I knew it wasn't coming back. There was a silence in the depth of my soul, a listening that I'd never been aware of before.

At mother's memorial, a large gathering of people came to express the impact that Teddy had made on their lives with her generosity of spirit, resources, and heart. One man summed it up when he said, "I came to Teddy a broken boy. I had been thrown away like a piece of trash. She took me in and she loved me, taught me I had value. I asked her why one day and she said, 'Because you're worth it.' She truly saved my life." It appears that Teddy is still expressing that love to humanity.

Because of my psychic nature and intense love for my mother, I expected to have some kind of communication with her. After all, I'd had dream-visions of my father, in-laws and some friends after their passing.

92

However, nothing could have prepared me for the intensity of what occurred nineteen days after she died and continued on for approximately three years.

I was in an airplane headed to NYC to visit two of my daughters, one of whom was pregnant. She had only known for a few weeks, and we were all so excited at the beautiful news, especially coming so soon after such a loss in our lives. In fact, my daughter had asked Mother to "Ask the angels to send her a baby" just a few weeks before her transition. Mother said she would, and lo and behold, it had already occurred!

As I gazed across the glorious sky, the pain of her absence prompted me to say in my mind, "Mother, is there any distance for you?" The joy of her presence enveloped me, and then came her voice. It was startlingly clear and unmistakably hers. She gave no preface to her statements, and simply started talking to me as if we were in the middle of a conversation. The experience of hearing her voice can best be compared to what it's like when you hear a song in your head – the music, lead singer, backup singers, lyrics and all. Rarely do we question how music flows through our minds in such a way- in fact; it's a common event for most people. I can only say that in the same manner, Mother's voice sounded as real and felt as natural to me as it had when she was alive. It seemed to echo both in my mind and all around me, but no one else seemed to hear it!

At first, I felt I was having a personal conversation with her, and we talked about some things pertinent to my own life. Then the topics branched off into more universal themes. I was not alarmed or frightened – in fact I was thrilled, comforted and excited. Looking back, I suppose I thought that it would be a one-time encounter on the plane that would end when we landed. I didn't really analyze it too much at the time, but simply wrote down what I was hearing so I wouldn't lose the treasure I knew I was being given.

It wasn't to be a one-time encounter. For many months I was bombarded with a series of conceptual realizations, which were accompanied by Mother's voice giving detailed explanations, examples, analogies, methods, affirmations and prayers. Most of the information came unbidden, flooding my being when I was otherwise occupied or in a relaxed state of mind rather than when I deliberately tried to seek it. In fact, on the rare occasion I attempted to induce it, I rarely received anything. I soon realized that I needed to carry a notepad around with me so I could be ready to write down what I was hearing, for I found that if

I didn't respond immediately, I would usually have no memory of what had been said, or at best just a vague notion of the concept with no substantial accompanying details. I also found that the best way for me to record it was to write it out by hand. Then it would come in a great rush, as if it had a mind of its own, much sloppier and larger than my own writing, but more accurate. A few times I tried using a tape recorder or typing on a computer, but the handwriting proved to be the strongest medium by far.

The inspiration always began with Mother's voice, but sometimes it would shift and the concepts would be impressed upon my mind in a flash, as if I'd seen a whole movie in a split second and knew the intricacies of the entire plot. Then, I would take this concentrated kernel of information and listen for her embellishments and examples so the concept could be fully fleshed out. Perhaps you have felt this before when you were suddenly struck with a profound understanding about something and just knew the complete story behind a certain situation or topic. Maybe it took just an instant of time, but in that instant was compressed a monumental degree of comprehension about a subject. Perhaps you felt you were being "hit between the eyes" with a single concept or even a whole set of principles, and afterward you couldn't believe that you hadn't grasped before what was now so obvious, clear and simple. This is the manner in which most of the material was received.

Although some of the basic concepts she talked about were familiar to me, there were just as many that I could never have dreamed of, had never heard of, and certainly had never looked at from that particular point of view. They puzzled and astounded me even as they appeared on the page before me. Because Mother was a school teacher and counselor, she used examples involving children and educational practices as her primary theme. I can't tell you how many people who have read the books have said, "That's your mother all right. It sounds just like her," for Mother had a somewhat formal way of speaking due to her Australian heritage, and her conversation was always peppered with humorous sayings.

I have learned through this experience that when conditions are right and a certain level of openness and trust exists, spiritual Team members can and will break the bonds of what is considered "normal" human experience to bring forth something they know it is time to divulge. As Mother teasingly put it to me, they know "how to make hay while the sun shines!" In keeping with her usual playful attitude, she also said at one time, "Isn't this FUN?" Truly, joy is Mother's trademark, and I felt that joy and an incredibly brilliant kind of energy all throughout the time I was writing these books.

The flow of information brought with it a flow of energy as well. During the years of writing, I was literally "high on life." I required very little sleep, was joyful and peaceful, and could burn the midnight oil as needed. Best of all, I was free of the bodily pain that had weighed me down much of my life. All the problems I'd had with headaches, ruptured disc pain and fatigue faded away. I felt lighter, freer, happier, and younger! I was healed on every level - emotionally and physically. Grudges, unforgiveness, and outbursts of anger dissolved as if they had never existed. I felt pure love for all of humanity. The world of Nature transformed before my very eyes. A tree erupting from the Earth was seen as an incredible creature of wisdom and divinity, as if I'd never seen it before. I'm reminded of the Beatles song, "There were birds on a hill, but I never heard them singing, no I never heard them at all, 'til there was you." Color, sound, and beauty were magnified beyond description. It was as if I were living on a new planet!

In addition to this awareness and buoyant health was a feeling in my forehead of tingling warmth. I had felt this sensation from time to time in my life, especially when meditating, but usually it was brief. I know now this was the third eye stimulating my spiritual receptivity. This feeling came and stayed for three years. At times it would fade a little, but not completely. It was always present during the writing process, and sometimes it became so intense I felt woozy. To this day, it appears often as I do my spiritual work.

Four books of insights called "*The Team: A Mother's Wisdom from the Other Side*" were birthed from these years of writing. The first book was written and released within three months after that fateful plane ride, and the others followed shortly after. The style of Book One is my Mother's alone. Anyone who knows her who has read the books says, "That's her all right!" But the other books took on another tone. I became aware that because I had opened myself so fully to my mother, trusting the source and no longer afraid of the process, other members of the spiritual group to which she belongs, our spiritual "Team", were now able to come through. Subsequent books have the voice of scientists, physiologists, and various perspectives by distinct personalities. Some chapters are very playful, some more analytical, and some more religious. The four books explore such topics as: The Quality and Quantity of Consciousness, The

Wheat from the Chaff, Reciprocal Influences, Nothing to Forgive, The Agreements, Preparing for Your Own Death, and so much more. All are based upon the overriding theme, "You are not alone. You're not even functioning as one person. Nobody is. For you are a member of a team, a spiritual team as close to you as breathing." The books are a testimony unto themselves, and describe much more about the relationship I had with my mother and the "supernatural" events we shared throughout our lives together. They are certainly the crowning manifestation of a connection to the Other Side that began in my childhood.

Without a doubt, connecting with the Team and being their scribe has been the ultimate experience of my lifetime. In addition, though, many miraculous events that have happened in connection to other people are just as meaningful to me, for they provide evidence of how real this connection is for everyone. For this reason, I want to share with you two other experiences that are extremely evidential in nature and were witnessed by people other than myself.

The first story is about my former husband, Eddie. I love to tell people about the events surrounding Eddie's death because I that know my telling will bring comfort and strength to those who hear about the beautiful nature of his passing. Despite the fact that he and I were divorced, we remained close friends (we met at age 14) and our four daughters and I were all involved in his care over the years. He had been disabled for many years, enduring a liver transplant as well as a kidney transplant, astounding his doctors with his stamina. But his strength had run out. Both his heart and his lungs were weakened by the years of medication and surgery. He'd been in and out of the hospital for months and was back on dialysis. He was dying of congestive heart failure.

One morning, I got a call from him. "Sweetheart," he said. "I died and I came back!" Then he put the nurse on the phone who verified he'd been found unresponsive and they had used chest compressions and medication to revive him. Eddie was eager to talk to me about it, and I was just as eager to listen. I knew that his background was very traditional in the area of religion. He'd been raised in a Christian home and while he respected the experiences I'd had, his outlook on life had remained pretty much the same. He claimed to be "a Christian who believes in reincarnation." I hurried to the hospital and sat by his bedside as he continued with his story...

"I was floating out of my body through a deep darkness, but I wasn't afraid. I knew without a doubt I had died. I ascended towards a light and when I arrived at the light, it was coming out around the edges of a door. The door opened and an enormous form stood there, made of light. I couldn't see details, it was all light. I knew that this was Jesus. He said, "Eddie," and I said, "Yes, sir?" He said, "It's not time for you to be here yet. Go back." I said, "Yes, sir." Then he said, "And you know how you've always called me The Naz?" (The Naz was short for "The Nazarene', a phrase used by a comedian that Eddie liked. He often said to me, "Me and the Naz are on good terms. Don't worry about the kids, I've been talking to him!") Eddie felt a little embarrassed about that fact, and hung his head as he again said, "Yes, sir." Jesus laughed a little and said, "The Naz - I like that!" Then he told him, "Go back now, and don't be afraid. Because I'm always in your heart." Eddie understood this to mean that he was both figuratively in his heart and literally in the tissue of his dying heart. He floated back peacefully and awoke to the crash cart team working on him.

That night, I sat with Eddie in his hospital room until 1 AM. He told me the room was full of angels and he was afraid that he was dying for sure. I reminded him of what Jesus said, and told him, "If there are angels here, they are either here to heal you or to take you to heaven. So there's nothing to fear." He agreed and went to sleep.

The next day, he told me that he wanted to be disconnected from everything. If he lived, so be it. If he died, he was ready. They moved him to the hospice ward and shortly after arriving there he told me, "Sweetheart, I won't be here tomorrow. Something has changed." He refused morphine, claiming he had no pain, and rested peacefully, dozing off and on, talking with us very lucidly, listening to jazz music and watching TV. At one point, he said, "Turn off the TV. I can't see anything anyway because of that big tunnel swirling in front of it. Do you see that?" I did not, and yet I knew what it must be - the tunnel spoken of by people having an NDE! It amazed me that he was seeing this at a time that proved to be ten hours before his death, right there in the middle of the hospice room. I knew that Eddie didn't know about NDE accounts or any details of other people's experiences. That kind of information was just not on his radar.

Our daughters and I rotated being with him over the next twenty hours or so. I had gone home for a break when they called me to come back. "He seems different," they said. At that time, I was lying on my bed, so I said a quick prayer before heading back. I thought about his mother, who had died years ago and said to her, "Louise, please help Eddie cross over. Please help him have no pain and fear…"

When I arrived back at the hospice center, the girls had an amazed look on their faces. "He's been talking to his mother!" they said. "He can see her and she's urging him to go." Apparently, Eddie had argued with her saying, "But I love all these people here, mother!" The girls told him that I was on my way, and it seemed to them he was hanging on, waiting for me. Then, he called out, "Neville! What are you doing here, man?" Neville was his friend who had died while they were both in kidney dialysis ten years ago.

I had five minutes with him before he took one last deep breath and passed. In that time, he opened his eyes, smiled and kissed me. The look on Eddie's face was pure peace and relaxation at the moment of death. None of us had any doubt that what he had seen and heard before his passing was authentic. From his NDE to the angels in the room, from the tunnel to his mother and friend who accompanied him onward, he was guided and protected. I can honestly say that being allowed to witness his passing with our children was a tremendous gift to us all.

Another experience I would like to share with you is undoubtedly the most amazing one to occur in my 64 years, and it happened recently - in December, 2016.

In early December, I had two vivid dreams about a week apart. In the first dream, my sister Kelly and I were talking about a woman who had died in a car accident. Kelly said, "Just think, if she had done anything differently, even just paused for a second, she wouldn't have been at that place at that time."

As I walked away from Kelly, she called my name and when I turned to her, she said, "See? You just paused and it changed your destiny."

In the next part of the dream, I was floating out of my body along a street. It was dark but I could see the lines down the middle of the road. There in the middle of the street stood Eddie, looking radiant and young, in a beautiful blue long-sleeved shirt. He hugged me and said, "Sweetheart! I earned this."

I said, "Earned what?"

He said, "To be the one to meet you."

I responded, "You mean I'm dead?"

And he said, "Yes! And I'm going to take you and show you - "

But I interrupted him with an adamant "No! I can't leave yet. The grandchildren need me, and I won't go." Immediately I was over my granddaughter's bed and realized she could not feel my touch. Again, I stated with absolute certainty, "I am not going to die now. I refuse."

Needless to say, this dream puzzled me. I knew it to be a vision-like dream, not a typical dream, and I spent a lot of time thinking about the meaning of it. A week later, I dreamed again that I was dying. This time, I was watching spirits float through the air as they passed on, and I felt myself joining them. I said, "All right, if this is what must be, if it's my time to go, I accept." Immediately I was moved by a strong current upward at a fast pace. It was blissful and beautiful, but again my soul cried out, "No! It's not time for me to leave, I cannot go!" I returned by exerting my will and forcing the current that was carrying me away to curve back down to the Earth. I landed on the ground and walked into a house where I began to inspect every corner of it, making sure "everything was complete" in it. In my hand was a list of things that had to be done.

Another week passed, and I decided to visit my cousin, Lisa, who lives here in town. I described to Lisa these dreams and we talked for hours about life and our spiritual pathways. At 11:00 pm, I headed back home. There was little traffic to deal with, and for no particular reason I decided to cut through an area where a metaphysical church my mother and I once attended is located. Driving past it was not a conscious goal, but that's where I ended up. I'd looked at the church many times over the past thirty years since it closed down, and while it is now a private residence, I never saw anyone coming in and out of the place. The building is in an affluent area and always looked beautifully maintained but basically inactive.

This night, however, to my great surprise, the porch was ablaze with light! There were about fifteen people standing on the porch, some on the steps of the house, some on the big veranda, and a few sitting in chairs. They seemed elderly at first glance because most of them had white hair shining under the lights. I slowed down in front of the house, gazing at the pretty spectacle and wondering what these older people were doing there at this late hour. Everything around the house and street was quiet and dark. I thought to myself how it reminded me of all the times the members of the church had stood around on the porch after the service, chatting and drinking coffee. It was a moment of beauty for me, and I continued on my way.

I drove the length of one more house when a woman in a car came speeding in front of me, missing my car by a millimeter. She never even saw me. There was no horn, no swerve, and no screech of tires. We both just drove on, having been spared a calamity. It happened so fast, I didn't even have time to feel a rush of adrenalin in my body or a leap of fear in my stomach. After driving a few more minutes, I pulled over and absorbed the event. The car was headed towards the driver's side, going about forty miles an hour. Had she hit me, I believe she would have driven straight through me. But I had paused, and it had changed my destiny. I had paused because the lights and people on my former church porch was such an amazing sight to see.

Not long after, my friend Kathy came to visit. She took one listen to the story and said, "Those weren't people on that porch. They were angels. Let's go talk to the owner." We drove to the house and knocked on the door. No one was home, but we could see through the window that there was a stair rider attached to the banister for someone disabled to descend and ascend the stairs. My plucky friend was not going to be deterred. "Let's talk to the neighbors," she said, so we headed next door.

A gentleman and his girlfriend answered the door, and although the moment felt awkward, Kathy and I managed to relay the story. I knew the exact date and time of the event, so we asked if the neighbors might have had a party that night. He said it was very doubtful as he had rarely seen any activity there. An older man and his disabled wife lived there; the wife was bedridden upstairs. We talked further and he divulged that he was a brain surgeon at the Mayo Clinic, and while most doctors were skeptical about apparitions, NDEs and so forth, he was not. He said his own father had appeared to his nephew in a flesh-and-blood appearance. He personally could not believe the mystery of the human brain was not created by intelligent design. His girlfriend kept smiling and saying, "Yes, I believe. These were angels."

As we all stood chatting on the porch of the doctor's home, the owner of the church house pulled up. Kathy and the doctor hurried to his car and within the space of a few minutes, they were smiling and waving at me. "No party! No party!" they yelled. As the conversation progressed, they learned that the man and his wife never had gatherings, and certainly wouldn't have had one at 11:20 pm on December 18th. It was an impossibility. The five us left the conversation with nothing left to say except how deeply our faith in divine intervention had been fortified.

Four months later, as I write this out, I am still in awe of such a remarkable event. I am searching deeply for more guidance as to the next phase of my life. What was on that list of things for me to accomplish? Why was I shown my pending death and why was my insistence on staying honored by an entire porch-full of angels? No doubt, sharing these happenings with readers such as you is part of the plan.

A lifetime of evidence has given me a certainty about the nature of life and death. We are all here to contribute to the evolution of humanity and the Earth by pursuing our own spiritual evolution. This is a process that occurs by serving others compassionately and without judgment, by remaining humble and grateful, and by seeking an authentic, loving connection with God, whatever that may be to you. We are all just passing through. Time is fleeting, life is precious, and the chance to fulfill our assignments is not something to squander. My prayer is that your lives will be enriched and filled with hope by hearing of these events and that you will walk onward and upward with a spirit of courage and willingness to serve your Team as well. No greater happiness can be found than this, my friends. Let us work together as One.

About Frances

Frances was born in Guantánamo Bay Cuba to an Australian mother and American father who met during World War II. On October 9, at the age of 86, Gloria Crystal "Teddy" Key passed away at her Florida home. Nineteen days later, her lilting Australian voice began to communicate with her eldest daughter, Frances, about the scope and wonder of her new perspective from the afterlife state. Frances experienced an afterlife communication with her which began the most astounding writing project of her life. The rush of information she received from her mother was so intense, it resulted in a series of books, "The Team: A Mother's Wisdom from the Other Side." This remarkable collection of insights, written in less than a year and divided into four books, has astounded friends, family and a growing circle of readers with its unique analogies, with, depth of wisdom, and unusual outlook on the human experience. theteambooks.com

Love Never Dies
My Son in the Afterlife

Elisa Medhus, MD

Erik was born on September 21, 1989 at 3:00 in the afternoon. He greeted the world without a whimper. Instead of howls of protest at the bright lights and cool air, he seemed content to take in his surroundings peacefully. Until he was around thirteen, he was such a happy boy. He loved all things manly: motorcycles, military paraphernalia, race cars, and guns. He also adored women of all sorts. Even as a four-year-old, he would lavish them with admiration and affection.

Erik had his struggles, though. He suffered from learning difficulties making school an unwelcome and often overwhelming undertaking. Despite our encouragement and understanding, his academic shortfalls ravaged his self-esteem. To make matters worse, he also suffered from Tourette's—so his odd tics and mannerisms left him vulnerable to unkind remarks and school bullies. He was finally diagnosed with severe Bipolar Disease, a vicious monster that took him to the darkest caves of depression from which he eventually never surfaced.

Then came that horrible Tuesday, October 6, 2009, that deep chasm that tore my life into two parts—the "before" and the "after"—when Erik killed himself at twenty-years-old.

No pain is as great as losing a child. It was like an atom bomb blew up, shattering our home and our hearts. My entire family and I plunged into a state of numbness. We were shaken by a grief so profound; each minute seemed like an eternity. From making the funeral arrangements, choosing a casket and burial plot to deciding what clothes he should wear in his perpetual sleep was an agony that clawed angrily at my heart. Every decision was gut-wrenching and insurmountable. All I wanted to do was lie down in a corner and sob.

What made it worse for me is that I didn't have any beliefs about what might have happened to him. For one, I'm a physician whose entire world is structured in science, and science taught me that, unless it could be perceived by one or more of the senses or measured with an instrument, it didn't exist. I could do neither with Erik, so what was I to think? What's more, I was raised by intransigent atheists. These two things made it impossible for me to answer what would become the most important questions in my life: "Does my son still exist? If so, where is he? How is he?"

In all the tragic turmoil; however, it was Erik who came to provide us with comfort. The second night after his death, he came to my husband in an uncharacteristically vivid dream. In that dream, they were both standing near my husband's, Rune's new Ford F-350, a truck that my son drooled over with great pride. Then Erik said in joyous excitement, "I feel so wonderful! I'm so light and free. It's an amazing feeling. Here, Pappa, feel." And when Erik reached out to grab his father's hands, Rune was overcome with a sense of intense euphoria unlike any sensation he's had before. It was a feeling of joy, love, comfort, lightness, and freedom that simply cannot be described in our limited language as humans.

After a few moments, Erik let go of Rune's hands, leaned toward him and said, "This is what I felt like before." Rune then felt the deep despair and darkness that had long tormented his son. The world felt heavy and unwelcoming. Rune knew Erik was trying to convey that he was fine, in fact happy for the first time in years. From that moment, healing for our family had begun.

Erik's grandfather, José, had a similar experience. Three days after Erik died, my militantly atheist father called me, voice filled with panic. He explained that he was sitting in his chair reading the paper when he looked up to see Erik standing in front of him. Then Erik turned into the little boy version of himself and crawled onto his grandfather's lap and snuggled against his chest.

My father felt, without a doubt, that Erik's presence was real. He felt the warmth of his grandson's small body and the love that emanated from his presence. Erik's visit challenged the very foundation of the staunch beliefs my father had held for decades. "I'm so startled! I don't know what to believe!" he cried. My father wasn't the sort of person who would make this kind of story up to lift my spirits. In fact, he was so deeply rooted in his atheism that his first words to me after I told him Erik had died were: "I'm sorry, Elisa, but Erik is going to turn to dust."

That was the crack—the beginning of my journey from skeptic to believer. First, I voraciously devoured everything I could on alternate dimensions, near death experiences, studies on consciousness, and the quantum physics behind these. Meanwhile my family and I experienced things that suggested that Erik still existed in the afterlife. For example, a week after he died, my second oldest, Michelle, and I were walking toward Erik's room when she felt his presence strongly. She picked up a camera that happened to be on a nearby table and started snapping pictures. When we looked over the photographs, one caught our interest. It revealed a bright orb with a comet-like tail giving the appearance of following me as I rounded the doorway to Erik's room.

I was so intrigued that I had a photographer expert analyze it. He brought the gamma down to produce a filtered image and concluded, based on that image, that the orb was its own light source, even casting light on nearby structures.

Soon after, we began to experience what we could only chalk up to Erik's pranking, which he was widely known for in our family. Water faucets would turn on and deadbolts would lock as we looked on. Airsoft BBs would appear at the ceiling and drop to the floor. Unplugged appliances would turn on. Objects would suddenly become hidden.

Eventually, the evidence became all but indisputable. About three months after his death, Erik called me on the telephone. When the phone rang, I screened the call assuming it might be one of those annoying telemarketing calls and ignored it. After what seemed like an exasperating eternity, the answering machine picked up, and I heard Erik's voice say, "Mom, it's me, Erik. It's me!" I ran to pick up the phone, but I was too late. The odd thing was that it was a twelve-digit number, and when I tried to call it, it wasn't a working one. Also, there was no message left on the answering machine. Message count: zero.

And then I had my first Erik sighting. As I started to lay my head on the pillow to go to sleep one night, I saw him at the foot of my bed jumping from one side to the other, over and over again, seemingly oblivious to my presence. On the left side, my deceased sister, Denise, sat and watched him with a big grin on her face. I followed him with my gaze, thinking about how surreal the moment was. Clearly, I was awake. How could this be? Then, all of a sudden, Erik turned to me, shock registering on his face. He said, "Mom, you can see me!" Then he fell into my arms and hugged me. The hug felt solid just like the many hugs we had shared when he was alive. Moments later, he disappeared, leaving me in a state of both astonishment and bliss.

Still, after each of these experiences, time would pass and doubts would creep in. My science background and atheist upbringing would take over. "Did I imagine it all? The Erik sightings and experiences, maybe they were all in my head?" I couldn't rest without knowing what happened to Erik: "Is there life after death? Is he safe?"

My questions tormented me, and I began my search for a gifted medium who could give voice to my son. In a way, I found this funny because before Erik's death, if someone had mentioned the word "medium," it would have conjured up the image of a gypsy hunched over a crystal ball. Nevertheless, I had read rather convincing articles on controlled studies on mediums, and I also read that many parents seek the help of a medium to connect with their child, often out of desperation. I knew that there are many mediums out there that are frauds, con artists, so I had to be very careful in my search.   After a few weeks, I received a hot tip from a friend of mine who claimed to have had several sessions with a medium named Jamie Butler that were uncannily accurate. I booked a session for the following week and discovered that I had found what I was looking for. In our sessions, she said, "Your son is here and he says he killed himself." I was poleaxed. I never gave her any information other than my name and credit card number. She went on to say that he shot himself, what kind of gun he used, that he was sitting at his desk in his bedroom when he pulled the trigger and that he was wearing a white shirt with three-quarter length blue sleeves. She also perfectly captured Erik's irreverent personality and sailor talk. Repeating his raw language often made her grimace and blush.

Since that first session, we've had dozens more. At first, I asked personal questions like, "Why?" "Did we do anything wrong?" and "Could we have done anything to save you?" I would also ask him about his death and death in general: what the afterlife is like, what it's like to live on the Other Side as a spirit and more. I even asked about bigger concepts like time, love, God, and the human experience. Other than the fact that I was actually able to hold conversations with my son, one of the best parts of each session was the chemistry between Jamie and Erik. It was clearly special, like an older sister and her pestering little brother.

During one of our channeling sessions, I happened to be videotaping it and I heard his voice. I recognized his characteristic verbal tic that sounded like he was clearing his throat, the way he said "breakfiss" instead of "breakfast," and his typical, incessant pacing. A mother knows the sound of her own child's voice. This was my Erik, without a doubt. To further confirm my belief, I had a sound professional analyze the voice, and he concluded that it did not belong to a human being. For one, it left no voiceprint. From that point forward, I knew Erik was still alive but in some other dimension, and I decided to continue to have a relationship with him.

Now, through mediums, I share everything that Erik says on my blog, Channeling Erik. I share many of our conversations in my book, My Son and the Afterlife. And through Jamie Butler, who serves as Erik's spirit translator, Erik wrote his own story, My Life After Death. It's an account of his journey from the moments before his death to the present. In it he shares intimate details about his own death, his life as a spirit, and the place he now calls home. Knowing these details has helped to ease the deep grief I used to have, and it has revealed to me that love truly knows no boundaries. Relationships never end if we are willing to open our hearts and minds beyond what we think are absolutes.

For instance, in one of our conversations I asked Erik to explain to me what happens when we die and he said, "To explain death in general does it an injustice . . . death is hand-tailored to the person's living belief system. Whatever you actively believe in—be it nothing, God, that you face your demons before you have joy, that you become a ghost—whatever it is, this is what's going to be laid out for you."

Erik goes on to say, "The physical body is the luggage that contains the spirit. When the body dies, it becomes a soul—it leaves the body. And that soul is then kind of contained in consciousness—that character you built, your personality. And so to move through these dimensions, to get to 'home' or Heaven, whatever the hell you wanna call it, it's gotta do that through that conscious element that you set up—that belief system that you set up—that's the tool to get you there."

I then asked, "Well, when you pulled that trigger, did you think there was going to be nothingness?

"I was kind of hoping for it. I mean, really, I was so desperate to get out of my skin. I was just hoping that I could . . . kind of what I imagine a person with a puppy or a baby, who has a lack of sleep [goes through]. I just wanted a good night's sleep. I just wanted some good, solid peace."

"Okay. When you pulled that trigger, what happened right after? First of all, did it hurt? "

"No, I don't remember any pain. I remember the sound, but I don't remember anything touching me. Just the sound. So, I think [I told you] how you get pulled from your body?"

"So, you felt a pulling sensation?"

"No, it was weird. It was like the lights went out. I had my eyes closed. I remember pulling the trigger. I remember I was quick about it. I didn't hesitate. I knew I was going to do this. This was the time. That was it. I didn't have any doubt about what I was doing. I wasn't conflicted. It's kind of like that state of mind."

"What were your emotions like when you saw your body? What did you feel?"

"Quiet. It was quiet. I had no pain. I didn't have any worries, and that was unsettling, because I hadn't felt that in a long time, like everything was in its right place."

Later in this same conversation, I ask Erik to describe how he felt after he knew he had died, he said, "When you slow down to go back through your memories, you see more. You do miss a lot when you're in the moment, like your eyes aren't big enough. I know I've told you before. I'm really sorry for you. I'm really sorry for Papa and for everyone else in my family. But I know there's one thing—I cannot apologize for my happiness."

That was difficult to hear but at the same time how could I not be happy for him? He was so miserable in life. In fact, my heart hurts when I think back on how he was bullied by his peers and teachers, how he suffered from his motor and verbal tics, how he struggled in school because of his learning disabilities, how he was a captive or his depression, which took him to the deepest depths of despair. How his friends treated him so poorly, often hanging up immediately when he called them, or inviting him over only to leave before he got there.

So yes, the loss was terrible—is terrible—yet the bliss and happiness Erik found on the other side was immense. This gave me solace. This gave me a reason to move through the grief, knowing we were and are still together, mother and son. Now, I can truly say that I no longer grieve over the "loss" of my son. I miss him, yes, but it's similar to the way a mother would feel when their child is studying abroad. She knows that eventually he or she will burst through the door with a sack of dirty laundry and will be united again.

Another profound conversation I had during my early sessions with Erik was when he described his "crossing over" from the earthly plane to the other side and his life review. Here is an excerpt from *My Life After Death* in Erik's own words:

"Everything seemed to happen quickly, like a blink—a long casual blink, like when you're tired. Suddenly, I felt warm, like I was in a really nice warm bath, but the warmth was all over me. I felt it on the inside; I felt it on the outside. I was absorbing the warmth, but I wasn't breathing it in. Well, I wasn't breathing at all, since spirits don't need oxygen, but you get the idea.

"Then I saw white light around me. Yeah, you do see a white light—no fucking joke—but it's not like the white tunnel of light people expect when you cross over. It was like I was moving across this huge white room with a white floor. For some reason, the light comforted me. It eased my nervousness a little bit, but not all the way. There were no smells or sounds, though, and I didn't see anyone. I thought there'd at least be some angel playing a harp on a cloud, but no—just silence and whiteness.

"Slowly, the white light started to turn into this glowing silvery mist with all sorts of beautiful hues that I don't even know how to describe. It was like I was going through a nebula but with a rainbow of many colors. I didn't feel like anything startling was about to happen, like I was about to be hit by a train, but at the same time there was this little lingering worry that I was going to end up in the wrong place, kind of like Harry Potter when he's getting sorted by the sorting hat. Everything was too much, too close, too crazy all of a sudden—that's what made me scared. It was then that I screamed for help.

"After I screamed, I started to see shapeless blobs in the light. Things started to change around me again. My logical mind said, 'You moved,' because I was still trying to think linearly, but it was more like a dimensional shift. Energetically, what happened to me was that I was coming out of the human dimension to enter a parallel one. Later, I learned that dimensions are all parallel but kind of smushed and swirled together. The blobs of light turned into what looked like people. So many people." 5

Erik then told me that the first person he saw was his Aunt Denise, my sister who also succumbed to suicide because of her chronic disability born from the ravages of her diabetes. He asked her, "Am I in Hell," and she laughed and said, "Why, because I'm here?"

Next, another spirit appeared behind Denise, his beloved paternal grandmother whom he called "Bestemor" which means grandmother in Norwegian. They exchanged hugs, then Denise took him by the hand and took him to a large room that had a long table and chair. Denise instructed him to sit down in order to experience his life review.

As for the life review, this is what Erik had to say about his experience: "Once the table of six spirits had shown up, I knew that I had entered the next step on whatever this journey was that I was on now. I was a little scared, but I also felt ready. They told me that I was about to enter my life review . . . The spirits told me that during my review, I was going to be shown things. I wasn't given the option to do or not do my life review. I was just told it was going to happen and that it would help me understand who I was and how to forgive myself. I didn't even realize that I was looking for forgiveness until they told me I'd be shown how to look for it.

"The table had a screen on it that I could look down on, but I could also see everything 360 degrees around me . . . All of a sudden, everything from when I was a tiny, tiny baby to the moment I died—the good, the bad, and the ugly—came flying at me from all directions. First came my birth. I felt myself being squeezed out of my mom. I felt her joy and her pain. I felt my family's excitement. What followed was intense, to say the least. As my entire life unfolded before me, I was not only experiencing every single moment I ever lived but I was also observing and feeling what everybody else in my life went through in reaction to whatever I said or did to them. I felt their joy, their hurt, their disappointment—shit like that. I saw their reactions to when I lied, when I withheld my feelings, when I didn't help someone who needed me, when I was mean, when I gave too much and when I gave too little.

---

[5] Erik Medhus and Elisa Medhus, *My Life After Death: A Memoir From Heaven* (Hillsboro, OR: Beyond Words/Atria, 2015) 44-45.

"I also got to see and feel all the good things I said and did too. Seeing how everyone chose to interact with my choices was fucking powerful. Not only could I feel the emotions they had in response to my actions but I could actually see things from their perspective. It was like I was them. I got everything down to the smallest little detail, like how many times that person blinked and how many times they swallowed in their lifetime—all experienced simultaneously. That's how detailed it was . . . .

"From that part of my review, I learned that responsibility is never only on one person's shoulders. It's meant to be shared . . . My life review made me feel like I had been cast in a role and played it, and when it was over, I got to read the reviews, knowing I was just a character in the play that was my life. It's weird . . . because I knew that whatever choices I'd made were just a part of that play. As a human, I was playing myself. As a spirit, I truly am myself, and I'm looking back at the part I played."6

* * *

From Erik's death, I learned several things. For one, I found out that I am stronger and braver than I thought I was. With the help of my very supportive family, I was able to dig down deep and find the courage I needed to turn something tragic and dark into something positive and uplifting. Second, I learned that death is not the end. When we die, we simply shed our bodies along with all physical and mental illness and enter a parallel dimension full of wonder. Third, because of that, I now see that relationships don't need to end just because someone we love dies. They can and must continue. Sure, they'll be different, but they'll also be just as real. Fourth, I understand the human experience, the answers to those ever-coveted questions: "Who am I and why am I here?"

Here's a conversation between Erik and me when I asked him, "What are we?"

"We're part of a big field of energy—of consciousness made of energy. We're individual segments of that consciousness, but we're also the whole—kind of like a hologram—which can be both the whole and parts of the whole at the same time. In the simplest of sentences, we are sentient energy."

---

6 Erik Medhus and Elisa Medhus, *My Life After Death: A Memoir From Heaven* (Hillsboro, OR: Beyond Words/Atria, 2015) 55-58.

"What is our purpose as parts and as the whole of that field of consciousness?"

"We try to seek lower entropy, both as separate units and as part of the whole. We project to the whole what we do individually. We are here to evolve to a higher level."

"So what is that, actually? I know lower entropy means lower disorder or chaos, but what does that mean in practical terms? What's the endpoint?"

"For one thing, we try to get to the point where we stay in Heaven to work with others who are still on the earthly plane, striving to evolve themselves."

"Okay, I can see that as the endpoint for us as individual souls, but what about the whole? What's our goal as the entire field of consciousness, as all the souls put together?"

"We seek to become love—unconditional love—as individuals and for the universe as a whole, for each soul to embrace. That's the lowest entropy. That's the endpoint."

"I've heard someone describe us as consciousness moving through various perspectives experiencing ourselves."

"Damn! Who wrote that?"

"I don't remember."

"Yeah, Mom, that's who we are. That pretty much nailed it."

Erik also said what scientists are only just now realizing that our souls are made of neutrinos, very tiny particles that were discovered because they were found to pass through lead. He went on to tell me that these neutrinos are carriers of information. In a sense, we are information. We're sentient information that is self-aware.

Erik describes death in terms of physics, too. He said that our neutrino souls are attached to our bodies within the hollow space of these tiny intracellular structures called microtubules. These tubules are responsible for maintaining the structure of the cell and also play a part in cell division. As we begin the death process, the energy of our soul starts interacting with the energy in the hollow space of the microtubule and friction builds and builds. Eventually, the friction increases to a point where there's a spark, and at that spark, those two energies separate, disconnecting the soul from each cell, one by one. Interestingly, he said that in some cases, disconnection is delayed, and the friction builds well beyond the usual threshold. The result: spontaneous human combustion.

He added that this often occurs in those humans who have a hard time letting go of things. Hoarders would be an example.

In one of our sessions, Erik likened the human experience to cooking brownies. Where he is, they can get the concept of something like love, but as humans, we add in the experiential component. Consider the concept of temperature. You can get an idea of what hot is like, but until you experience cold, you don't completely understand. Where he is, he can see an image of a brownie along with its recipe, but to gain the experiential component, he must get into the kitchen, mix the ingredients into a batter, pour it into a plan, and bake it in the oven, perhaps burning a finger or two, but when the cooking is done and the brownies are cooled and frosted, that first bite is when he really understands what a brownie is.

This experiential component works because of contrast, and often that contrast causes human suffering. Our purpose is to understand all facets of love and to remember that we are that emotion called love. To understand that facet of love called forgiveness, you have to experience a life in which you are hurt or betrayed. In order to understand that facet of love called loyalty, you have to live a life where a friend or family member turns against you.

To understand that embodiment of love, you have to experience loss and death. However, that love is never lost—it's always been there and will always be there—as humans we have to experience contrast, the duality of life to realize what is ultimately true.

To all of you who have "lost" loved ones, know that they aren't really gone. They're still around, just without a body, and they're free of mental and physical illness. Therefore, you can continue to have a relationship with them, and they want you to. Maybe that relationship will be the same; maybe it'll be different, but it will be real and fulfilling if you choose to have it.

There are many ways to communicate with your loved one. You can do so through a medium as I did. You can even learn how to channel him or her yourself. Everyone has the potential to do so, and I have learned to do this myself. One simple way is to ask your loved one yes and no questions through the Hand Game. Designate one hand as your "yes" and the other as your "no." Then, with your hands spread apart, palms facing upwards, ask your question and wait. After a while, you'll pick up a different sensation in one palm. It might be a change in temperature, numbness, tingling, itching, pressure, a blowing sensation, etc. If your loved one has trouble making that sensation obvious, say, "Make it stronger" and repeat this until you're satisfied that you have an answer.

You can also have conversations with your loved one in your head or aloud. Sometimes they'll talk to you in what seems like your own voice, but it's easy to distinguish from your thoughts because they don't appear to belong to you. They seem to come out of nowhere. When I speak to Erik, I often hear him just behind my right ear. Sometimes he'll give me strong goose bumps to confirm that he is indeed talking to me. You can also add a tangible component to your conversations if you want. For example, I'll place two mugs of coffee on the table, one for him and one for me. I'll add napkins and spoons and put his photograph at his place setting so that I can see his image as I speak with him.

Many people communicate best with their loved ones in certain settings. For example, activities that are fairly automatic and calming like gardening or washing the dishes might make it easier to communicate with them. I channel Erik best in a warm bath or while I'm hiking in nature.

I talk to Erik nearly every day, and he continues to prank me from time to time, especially when I need the comic relief on days when I miss him most. Our relationship is different than the way it was when he was alive, though. It's no longer about trying to "fix" him, and the roles are reversed. He has become my teacher instead of me being his.

Since Erik's death, my entire family and I have grown spiritually. Not only do we understand that death is not the end, we know what to expect when our own time comes. As a result, we no longer fear death. We also understand who we are and why we're here and have gained a great deal of practical advice to get the most from our human experience. For example, we now know that we should open our hearts and live with vulnerability.

Vulnerability isn't a weakness. It's a position of strength, and it allows us to live a life of love. We've also learned that to be vulnerable, we need to feel first and think second and that takes being mindful of our own intuition, our heart space. Ordinarily, we humans do the reverse. We think a thought, and then that evokes and emotion and that emotion creates a choice or reaction. Instead, we must listen to our heart and be aware of the emotions we're feeling. Then that emotion will produce a thought and that thought will create a choice or reaction.

Once we're able to accomplish that, we can achieve one of the most important things as humans—emotional honesty. By listening to our heart, we can be emotionally honest with ourselves and others and that paves the way to a life of love.

Continuing a relationship with someone in the afterlife takes practice, consistency, and patience, but doing so will hopefully heal you as it has me. It will give you comfort knowing that your loved one will never leave you, that he or she is fine and that you will meet in the afterlife when your own time comes. Until then, know that love knows no boundaries, even death.

* * *

About Elisa

Elisa Medhus, a physician and mother of five, has practiced internal medicine in Houston, Texas for over thirty years.

After the death of her 20 year-old son, Erik, Dr. Medhus began journaling her grief on her blog, Channeling Erik. She knew that only in helping others could she heal herself. Because of her strong science background, she formerly viewed spiritual matters such as the soul's survival of death with skepticism, but once Erik began to communicate with family, friends and blog members, her entire paradigm shifted. After devouring various books on the quantum physics explaining the science behind spirituality, Dr. Medhus is no longer a skeptic. Now, she channels Erik through a medium, asking him questions about death, the afterlife and so much more. As her blog members join her in this journey toward spiritual understanding, Erik continues to offer not only his insight as an insider on the other side, but also adds some comic relief with his mischievous pranks. She shares her journey in her book, *My Son and the Afterlife: Conversations from the Other Side.* Erik has authored his own book, *My Life After Death: A Memoir from Heaven.*

In addition to her two books about Erik, Dr. Medhus is also the author of three award- winning parenting books: *Raising Children Who Think for Themselves, Hearing is Believing: How Words Can Make or Break Our Kids,* and *Raising Everyday Heroes.*

Talking to the Dead

Garnet Schulhauser

Little did I know how much my life would change that day in 2007 as I left my office in Calgary, where I had worked as a corporate lawyer for over 30 years.

As I strolled down the street that sunny afternoon in May weaving my way through the crowd of pedestrians, a disheveled homeless man jumped out of the shadows and stopped me in my tracks. His clothes were ragged and dirty, his beard was long and unkempt, and his long hair was greasy and stringy. He gave me a gap-toothed smile and looked intently into my eyes. His sparkling blue eyes infused my body with an amazing feeling of love, peace, and well-being, and we began a conversation that continues to this day—a revelatory dialogue that has transformed my life.

Up to this point my life was mostly on track. I was happily married to a remarkable woman who was a loving and devoted wife and mother. We had two bright and talented sons, both nearing the completion of their college degrees, and we took great pride in watching them mature into adulthood. I had a successful career as a corporate lawyer with a major law firm, while my wife cheerfully embraced all the challenges and rewards that arose from her profession as a public-health nurse. We lived in a nice house in an upscale neighbourhood and enjoyed the material comforts of life that came with financial prosperity. We were happy, healthy, and blessed with many good friends. Despite all of this good fortune, however, I yearned for something which had eluded me to that point in my life. I wanted the answers to all the big questions about life and death, which all too often roiled my mind, leaving me unsettled and dispirited.

Why am I here? I wondered. What, if anything, am I supposed to accomplish in my life? Did God select this life for me, or did the Universe assign it by chance? Is all the stuff I learned in Sunday school about God and the afterlife the real truth, or just a lot of hooey? Will God judge me when I die and send me to heaven or hell, based on how I lived my life? Does God really exist? Is it possible that when I die I will simply cease to exist—disappearing into nothingness? These questions swirled around in my mind for many years as I searched in vain for the "right" answers that would satisfy my mind and my heart.

Then that sunny afternoon in May as I strolled down the pedestrian mall near my office, the homeless man stepped out of the shadows, stopping me in my tracks. I had encountered homeless people on this mall many times before, and I had become quite deft at executing a quick side step to detour around them. But this homeless man was different—his amazing blue eyes penetrated my whole being, right down to the depths of my soul, and I was riveted to the spot, unable (and unwilling) to move.

I discovered that this man, whose name is Albert, was not really a homeless person, but one of my spirit guides in disguise, manifesting in a physical form no one else could see. He did this to answer all of my vexing questions and awaken me to my mission on earth. During the course of our discussions he told me, much to my surprise, that he and I were old friends who had known each other for a long time, although I had no recollection of our previous association. Our conversations were informal, like two friends chatting over a beer, and Albert did his best to give me answers I could understand and easily communicate to others. Albert had a sharp wit and keen sense of humour, and he was not above using sarcasm to chide me for my many human foibles. My dialogues with Albert are unforgettable, exhilarating experiences, and I am confident, without any doubt, that everything that Albert tells me is the "real" truth.

Albert takes me to the Spirit Side and other fascinating places in the universe in my astral body at night as I sleep, so I can chronicle what I see and hear. Albert recruited me to promulgate his messages for humanity in a series of books. I have written four books which fulfil Albert's desire that everyone should have the opportunity to read and understand his message to mankind. Albert's goal is to enlighten humanity with his revelations about our true nature as eternal souls, as we progress through the cycle of reincarnation on planet Earth. I find Albert's revelations to be comforting and inspiring and hope you will as well.

The rest of this chapter is from the first part of Chapter Seventeen, in my fourth book, *Dance of Eternal Rapture*. Here I describe a psychic reading I witnessed that connected the soul of a little girl with her parents on Earth. During one of my astral trips with Albert, I was able to view in the Akashic Records the tragic events that led to the brutal death of Emma, a sweet little seven-year-old who had been snatched by a perpetrator when her mother was distracted. Emma's parents were devastated and overcome with grief, but thanks to a friend they sought relief by arranging a reading with a respected psychic/medium named Alice,

From my perspective on the Spirit Side, I watched the events unfold as Emma's soul reached out to her parents to assure them she was alive and well, surrounded by relatives who had embraced her with unconditional love. With a lump in my throat, I heard Emma plead with her parents to stop grieving, forgive themselves, and get on with their lives, because she had left her incarnation when her soul was ready to exit. She explained that her short life had been planned beforehand to provide her parents with the difficult challenge of coping with the death of a child. It was heart-warming to see the relief her parents felt once they understood that Emma was still very much alive, and they would see her again when they made their own transition to the Spirit Side.

* * *

(From the book: Dance of Eternal Rapture.)

After publishing my first book, *Dancing on a Stamp*, dozens of people asked me if it was possible for them to communicate with their guides or other spirits like I did with Albert. I knew from my dialogue with Albert that it was possible for souls on the Spirit Side to communicate with people on Earth, and most often this happened through a psychic or medium.

The vast majority of humans cannot hear the voices from the Other Side because they do not have the psychic skills necessary to pierce through the veil to connect with the Spirit Realm. Albert told me that mediums are usually born with this talent thanks to a genetic quirk that gives them special powers. Many people who have this gift try to ignore their connections with the Spirit Realm to avoid being ridiculed by family and friends, while others work hard to hone this talent so they can help other people contact their deceased loved ones.

Albert had explained that when mediums read for someone they will receive verbal and/or symbolic communications from the souls closely connected to that person, like a parent, spouse, or child who has already passed from this life. The persons seeking the reading are often still grieving the loss of their loved ones and anxious to find out if they survived their physical death.

I accepted all of this, but I was curious about how this communication was arranged. So when Albert returned once again to my bedroom in the dead of the night, I asked him if I could observe one of these sessions from the Spirit Side. Albert agreed, and we began by accessing the Akashic Records to observe the background of events leading to the session with the medium I would be allowed to witness.

As we settled into one of the viewing rooms in the Hall of Records, I watched as Albert waved his hand over the holographic globe in the center of the room. The blue and white swirls soon gave way to the view of a park in a city in the Pacific Northwest of America about a year before in Earth time. The park was nestled near the edge of a forest of cedar and fir trees, interlaced with walking trials. It was a sunny afternoon in August, and the park was filled with families, couples strolling hand-in-hand, and joggers panting in the hot sun.

The scene in the globe zoomed in on a bench near the edge of the forest. A young lady, Angela, was watching her seven-year-old daughter, Emma, trying to catch butterflies in a little net affixed to a short pole. Emma had no luck catching any of the colorful insects, but she giggled cheerfully as she ran to and fro in hot pursuit.

Then Angela's phone emitted a short jingle, signaling an incoming text message. Reluctantly, Angela pulled her phone out of her pocket and focused on the text from one of her work colleagues. It was an urgent message requiring an immediate response from Angela. Several minutes later, Angela looked up to ensure her daughter was OK, but Emma was nowhere in sight. Angela quickly scanned the area by her bench and shouted Emma's name, her anxiety increasing with each passing moment.

And then panic began to grip Angela, as she feared the worst. Emma had never before wandered off on her own and this was totally unlike her. She sprinted around the park frantically, asking everyone in the vicinity if they had seen her little girl. Much to her dismay, no one had seen her daughter, and Angela had no idea where to search next. With tears streaming down her cheeks, she called her husband, Jeffrey, to plead for help. He arrived shortly, and the two of them expanded the search in ever-widening circles without any success.

They called the police and a search party was organized to scour the nearby forest. By now Angela was inconsolable and had to be sedated. Jeffrey left her at home with relatives as he continued to search through the night.

Two days later, Emma's body was found in a thicket of trees a couple of miles from where she was last seen. She had been sexually assaulted and strangled. Emma had wandered into the forest chasing a butterfly while Angela was focused on her phone. The perpetrator had snatched Emma when no one was looking and quietly disappeared into the forest.

In the days that followed, Emma's parents, especially Angela, were overcome with grief. Angela could not forgive herself for allowing Emma out of her sight, and she seriously considered suicide as a way to relieve her pain. Jeffrey, who was desperate to find relief for his wife, followed the advice of a friend and arranged for them to have a reading with a respected medium, Alice, who lived in their city.

They arrived at Alice's house at the appointed hour not knowing what to expect, but hoping to find comfort about what happened to their daughter. Alice invited them to sit in her living room and the reading began.

At this point Albert led me out of the Hall of Records and through the streets of Aglaia until we came to a low rectangular building with broad stone steps leading up to a large brass door. Inside we entered a meeting room with three souls seated in a row. Albert explained that these souls had gathered here to participate in the reading with Alice, and we were here to observe the action as they communicated with Angela and Jeffrey through Alice.

As soon as Jeffrey had arranged for the reading, his guides had contacted these souls to let them know they should be available to connect with Angela and Jeffrey during the reading, and they all eagerly agreed to participate.

Alice began by saying she was seeing the image of a little girl with a blond ponytail, wearing a blue tank top and white shorts and clutching a pink teddy bear. Alice asked Angela and Jeffrey if this had any meaning for them. Angela began to sob quietly as Jeffrey explained it was the image of their daughter, Emma, who had died recently. He said the pink teddy bear was her favorite stuffed toy that she slept with every night.

One of the souls in the circle, who looked like the little girl described by Alice, could wait no longer and began to speak with great excitement, with her words being relayed to Angela and Jeffrey by Alice: "Hi, Mommy! Hi, Daddy! I love you very much. I wish you could be here with me—it is so wonderful."

Angela fought to control her sobbing and finally managed to respond: "Hi, Sweetie. We love you to the moon and back. Are you alright? Are you happy? Do you have anyone there to look after you?"

"I am doing great, Mommy. I am very happy because this is a wonderful place where everyone loves everyone else and there are no bad people. When I first arrived here I was met by Grandma Joyce and Grandpa Andy, along with Aunt Betty and Uncle Tom. They enveloped me with warm hugs and smothered me with love. Then they led me into a beautiful meadow where I met my other relatives from Earth who had passed on before me, including a few I had never met before. They were all very nice, and they have been with me ever since, making sure my transition to the Spirit Side was as smooth as possible. I am in very good hands, Mommy, and I do not want for anything. Grandma and Grandpa are here with me now.

"I miss you and Daddy a lot, but I know we will be together again before too long. In the meantime, you and Daddy should stop grieving over me and get on with your lives. Although my human body died tragically, I survived my death and I am alive and well, waiting to be reunited with you and Daddy when it's your turn to come Home. Take comfort in knowing that I did not suffer at the end. I left my body before I was assaulted, and I did not feel any pain. My guides promptly escorted me to the Spirit Side so I did not have to watch the final moments.

"Do not be afraid of dying because death is merely a transition from one world to the next. Like me, you are eternal souls, and you will live forever. Please promise me you will stop mourning my death and start living your lives again. You both have many more experiences to enjoy on Earth, so forget about the past and treat today as your new beginning."

"I am so sorry, Emma, I failed you that day in the park. I can never forgive myself for letting you out of my sight. I hope you will be able to forgive me someday," Angela whispered between sobs.

"Of course I forgive you, Mommy, except there is nothing to forgive. You didn't cause my death; I left that incarnation when my soul was ready to leave. I incarnated as Emma to help you and Daddy experience the things you both needed for your evolution, and dealing with my tragic death was an acid test to see if you had the courage to overcome this adversity and emerge even stronger than before. Losing a child at an early age often leads to divorce, prolonged depression, or even suicide. Please don't fall into this trap.

"And above all, be sure to forgive yourself. You can't truly love and forgive others until you love and forgive yourself. Your journey on Earth will be happier if you accept love and forgiveness as your guiding principle, and you can best honor my memory by becoming a beacon of light for others to follow.

"It is time for me to go. I hope this contact has given you both some much-needed comfort. Know that I will always be watching over you until you return Home, sending you my love every day as you struggle to overcome all the challenges you will face. And any time you notice a white feather in your path, it will be a sign from me that I am always at your side. Farewell for now, Mommy and Daddy. I love you both dearly."

"We love you too, Emma," Angela and Jeffrey murmured in unison. They thanked Alice for connecting them with their daughter and returned home to start the next phase of their lives.

Emma turned to face me with a sparkle in her eyes. I didn't feel the need to say anything to her because there was nothing else to add to the heartfelt connection she had with her parents. She gave me a knowing wink and left with the other souls in tow.

I glanced at Albert to see what he planned for me next, but he seemed lost in thought, so I decided to take advantage of this pause in the action to ask him a question I had been planning to spring on him when the time was right. So I jumped in with my query before he had a chance to resume his agenda.

"Several people have asked me about near death experiences (NDEs), Albert, and there have been many books written about these paranormal incidents in recent times. Why do NDEs occur and what is their purpose?"

Albert responded after a thoughtful pause: "NDEs are just one example of a human epiphany designed to infuse hope and inspiration to those who are fortunate enough to experience this phenomenon. Sometimes these divine revelations happen to people in a dream, in deep meditation, or in times of great stress.

"NDEs typically happen when a person is clinically dead, or near dead, for a short while before a seemingly miraculous recovery. When these people awaken from their stupor, they can recall an out-of-body trip to the Spirit Side (or Heaven) where they encountered an assemblage of ethereal spirits, including deceased relatives, angels, religious deities, and sometimes even God.

"The common denominator for all of these experiences is that these people will undergo profound changes to their outlook on life once they leave the hospital. They will most often chart new courses for the remainder of their time on Earth, bolstered with the knowledge that they will continue to exist after death, and they have unfinished business to address. Thereafter their lives will have a new purpose that they will cheerfully pursue with love in their hearts—because they have seen the light and are no longer afraid of the darkness.

"NDEs are not identical, as they are tailored to suit the individual. A Christian may see Jesus Christ and his mother, Mary, to ensure this person will experience the things that will provide comfort and inspiration. Likewise, a Muslim may meet up with Muhammed to receive a message from Allah. In all cases, the out-of-body traveler will be enveloped in limitless, divine love, imbued with the knowledge that they will return to this blissful nirvana when their time on Earth is over.

"In most cases, these people will want to remain in Heaven because it is peaceful and permeated with love, in stark contrast to life on Earth. Invariably the spirits will persuade them to return to their human bodies because it is not their time to cross over, and they must complete their agendas on Earth. Sometimes their unfinished business relates to things they need to experience to advance their evolution, although in some situations they are encouraged to return to their human lives so they can help other people get the most out of their journeys.

"In every NDE the astral travelers are allowed to remember their trips to the Other Side, and the spirits they saw, to inspire them to live the rest of their lives as shining beacons for others to follow, even for those people who afraid to talk about their NDEs."

"But I have read about a few NDEs where the people traveled to frightening locations that reminded them of Hell," I interjected. "How do you explain these events?"

"As I said, in an NDE people will experience the things Spirit deems necessary for their journeys on Earth. The dreadful places these people encountered do not really exist—they were illusions created especially for them as something they needed to see. It was a 'stick' used to cajole them to reject the dark side of humanity in favor of love and light, because some people are more motivated by this tactic than by dangling a carrot in front of them."

"That reminds me, Albert, about something you said a while back about evil spirits. You told me the devil does not exist and there are no demons that plague our planet. You also said no spirits are inherently evil, even though some are mischievous. Can you explain what you meant by that?"

"The devil does not exist," Albert confirmed. "He is nothing more than a fictitious character invented by religious leaders to control the masses through fear. And there are no other demonic spirits who wreak havoc on unsuspecting humans, because all souls, when not physically embodied in the denser planes, are beings of pure energy who are intimately connected to the Source and to everyone and everything in the universe. And because the Source is love in its highest form, there is no room for anything on the Spirit Side other than wholesome, unfettered love.

"Evil, as you know it on Earth, does not exist in the Spirit Realm, and that term could never be applied to a soul over here no matter what it has done in its previous incarnations. The evil perpetrated by humans on Earth stays behind when their souls cross over to the Spirit Side, and the only baggage they bring back are the memories of their journeys on Earth.

"All souls are unique because they have all enjoyed different journeys since they spun out from the Source. As a result, all souls have distinctive personalities that have evolved over the course of their incarnations on the denser planes. And this diversity is what makes the Spirit Side so special, as we can celebrate the sui generis nature of all souls as individual aspects of the Source.

"If a soul had been quiet and somber during its lives on Earth, it will likely project a similar personality in the Spirit Realm. And a soul who had lived its lives on Earth with gusto and exuberance will likely be the life of the party on this side of the veil. By the same token, those souls who loved pulling off pranks and other mischief as humans will often continue this behavior after they cross over.

"These mischievous spirits take delight in slamming doors, turning lights off and on, and levitating furniture, in an effort to startle and unnerve those people who frighten easily. These spirits are not evil and they don't intend to cause any harm—they just enjoy a good laugh at the expense of superstitious humans. Unfortunately, some of their victims will believe they have encountered evil spirits, and they may suffer from nightmares as a result. There is no permanent harm done, despite the temporal discomfort felt by the timid.

"In some cases, this type of paranormal activity is arranged by a soul in its prebirth planning as an experience needed for its evolution, and it recruits other souls to carry out these ghostly undertakings at the appropriate time.

"On occasion, these preternatural incidents result from the psychokinetic abilities of certain humans who can move objects through the power of thought. Sometimes these humans use their powers consciously to achieve a desired result, but often this power is deployed subconsciously by people who are frightened or under a great deal of stress.

"So evil on your planet is not perpetrated by demons or evil spirits, because such entities do not exist. Evil on Earth is caused by humans who let their malevolent emotions rule their lives despite the best efforts of their souls and guides to steer them toward love and compassion. So while there are evil humans who dish out a lot of violence on your planet, their souls are not evil in any sense, and those toxic emotions do not continue in the Spirit Realm."

"What about all the stories I have heard about people being possessed by evil spirits and needing an exorcism to cast the demons out of their bodies?" I wondered.

"I think you have watched too many reruns of the Exorcist, and you are confusing the contrived horror created by Hollywood with reality. Like I said, there are no evil spirits, so it is not possible for them to invade a person's body, although I can understand why you would believe it to be possible. When you look at yourself in the mirror on Monday mornings, you would be forgiven if you thought you had become possessed by a dim-witted spirit who had snuck into your house over the weekend and permeated your whole body with the dreaded realization you were about to enjoy another fuzzy-headed start to a new week on planet Earth.

"But you would be wrong, because your usual 'Monday morning ecstasy' is entirely self-generated, and it is nature's way of telling you to get off your butt and do something useful for once in your life."

"Very funny, Albert. Except I like the possession theory better. In fact, you should consider possessing someone yourself. You could easily transform a happy, fun-loving human into a cranky old curmudgeon with no sense of humor."

Albert rolled his eyes and shook his head from side to side as though he was growing weary of engaging in a battle of wits with someone who had no ammunition. At last, I thought, I was able to get in the last word with Albert. But I sensed this wasn't the end of it, and I braced myself for his next salvo.

About Garnet

Garnet Schulhauser is a retired lawyer who lives near Victoria, on Vancouver Island, with his wife Cathy. He enjoys family gatherings with his two sons, their wives, and his three grandchildren. He very much enjoys the balmy climate on the west coast of Canada.

After practicing corporate law for over thirty years in Calgary with two blue-chip law firms, he retired in 2008 and his first book, *Dancing on a Stamp*, was published in 2012. Since the release of his first book, Garnet has been active with book signing tours and speaking engagements, and has been interviewed on over one hundred twenty radio talk shows broadcast from studios in the U.S, Canada, the United Kingdom, Ireland, and Australia.

Garnet's second book, *Dancing Forever with Spirit*, describes his next encounter with Albert who guided him on a series of astral adventures to visit the Spirit Side, the Akashic Records, distant planets with fascinating life forms, and a human civilization that made the shift to the New Earth.

His third book, *Dance of Heavenly Bliss*, continues the saga of his astral trips with Albert who took him to meet Gaia, the consciousness of Mother Earth, two of Earth's mythical creatures—a Sasquatch and an Irish fairy, a human civilisation on another planet that is ruled by women, and many fascinating souls on the Spirit Side who regaled him with tales of their lives on Earth, including Moses, Jesus and his mother Mary, Lucifer, and the goddess Athena.

Garnet describes his most recent astral travels in his fourth book, *Dance of Eternal Rapture*, including encounters with Mohammed, Buddha, Mary Magdalene, and Jesus, another conversation with Gaia, and a journey to Earth in a parallel universe where there is much less violence and strife due to a couple of quirks in the history of the planet.

When Garnet finished the manuscript for his fourth book, he began to search for new ways to help his fellow humans understand the meaning of life on Earth. Prompted by his wise spirit guide Albert, he enrolled in the Quantum Healing Hypnosis Technique ᴿᴹ Academy and became a QHHT® Level 2 Practitioner. With guidance from Albert, Garnet takes great delight in helping people connect with their Higher Selves to learn about their purpose for being on this planet, and the reasons for the successes, the failures, and the challenges they have experienced so far in their lives.

Visit Garnets Website for more information: http://www.garnetschulhauser.com

The Second Earth

Cyrus Kirkpatrick

To begin my chapter, I think it's best to understand a little about me: My name's Cyrus, a late-stage millennial who chronically travels, writes and pursues a life-long interest in metaphysical topics. This interest blossomed into a full study of life after death that led to building an afterlife educational community and publishing my 2015 book. My exploration of the beyond helped enormously upon the sudden deaths (or transitions) of various family members. This is my story.

While sudden spiritually transformative experiences compel other people, I believe my interest stemmed from practicality. I grew up completely isolated as a child (the youngest of 4,) in a Spanish-mission-style ranch deep in a sweltering Arizona desert. To only make my geographic exile worse, much of my time was spent avoiding constantly fighting parents—who were engaged in a perpetual (and entirely pointless) war of jealousy and possessiveness over their children. I had an excess amount of time to ponder big questions as I took long walks to avoid them—or isolated away on our 56k dial-up Internet modem, researching whatever interested me during the early days of search engines.

As I heard stories from my brother's weird dabbling in so-called "out of body experiences," my curiosity only grew. Life after death eventually entered my mind. It was a response to an overwhelming existential uncertainty that began around age 14. I remember wandering the desert landscape, as I so often did, and trying to comprehend the existence of *non existence.*

Well, trying to comprehend such a thing was similar to dividing by zero—it just couldn't happen. Every cell of my being rejected that feeling. It caused a literal sickness in my stomach. I also foresaw this issue causing enormous problems as I got older. Since I wanted my adult life to be marginally more enjoyable than my childhood, I knew I needed to focus on life and death.

I also knew that, unfortunately, life in my family was troubled: How long would my immediate family even be around before I had to bury them? Substance addictions run in all of our genes. I remember being barely past a toddler and becoming acquainted with the smell of cocaine in the house; a substance my mom insisted was a "medicine." In fact, she once applied it topically to a burn and it numbed the pain.

I learned far too early that, apparently, if the cocaine smells like "wet pavement" then it's a quality cut.

Of course, it was also consumed by my father and only added to his mania, paranoia and abusive traits.

My father insisted I never go to school or try to make a name for myself or do my own thing. He wanted me to live as a country "ranch hand" for the rest of my days—shoveling horse manure and, I assume, wearing overalls with a piece of straw dangling from my teeth. Even in some parallel dimension where my brain was made of mush and this idea appealed to me, I knew it wouldn't be sustainable because his addiction issues would eventually catch up with him and he'd either end up dead or destitute. It did not help that he jealously guarded his small fortune— refusing to so much as sign a will or distribute anything among his children.

I put my foot down and made a life for myself despite facing enormous resistance, which means I escaped the ranch, enrolled in (and graduated from) university, found a job, rented a place to live and began my own path. To cut years of subsequent drama short: he did lose everything. Ten million-dollars of property and every last dollar he possessed went up in smoke.

Afterwards, I dealt with the enormous stress of watching my parents survive on marginal income and continue to feed their addictive issues. At one point, since no one would rent to them, I smuggled them into an apartment where they hid from the owners and could only leave at night when neighbors wouldn't see them. Later they were evicted from two rental homes, and in their third they ended up with no water and a $3,000 bill to turn it back on. Dealing with this train wreck was a constant nightmare.

Nonetheless, I trudged forward in my own life. I discovered the banality of working traditional jobs during and post-college. I focused all my effort on becoming an entrepreneur. I started to funnel my strengths into the craft of writing plus freelance work. This sustained myself well enough, and even allowed me to work on the road as I traveled, but it never provided enough money to magically cure my family's problems. My parents continued to struggle and in many ways my brothers did, too.

The fear of death became enormous, and this was almost entirely in relation to my mother. I knew her health was on a downward spiral. My father was making no attempt to wean her from alcohol abuse, and so her life became a ticking clock as I watched her good health deteriorate from her face. Worst of all, she just wasn't living a fraction of the life she deserved in her 60s. An artist of great talent, her pen and ink wildlife work decorates the personal office of Jane Goodall and was once featured across Arizona. Extremely creative, inventive and full of imagination, all her potential was crushed in the throes of a co-dependent relationship. Almost my entire childhood and adult life was spent trying to "rescue" her—to bring her back to an independent lifestyle and help her achieve the life she deserved. However, she never put in the effort to try to help herself.

By the time I moved to Los Angeles, California in 2013, I'd all but given up. I left the constant struggle of Arizona; however, the issues with my family continued to haunt me. Restless nights were spent fearful of my mom. With every extra bit of money I'd fly back home and try in vain to "help," only to find a rapidly deteriorating situation.

Sudden Contact with the Beyond

In 2014 after settling into Los Angeles, the astral world's existence started flooding into my life. It started with odd out-of-body experiences in the morning. I'd find myself sitting up in my bed and reaching for my alarm clock, only to find my hand was see-thru and passing straight through it. Logically, as I had learned so much about the physics of the other side through constant reading of metaphysical literature, I knew what was happening—yet it still seemed like such an unbelievable occurrence.

Just a few days later, I felt the familiar electrical tingle down my spine as once more my body was disconnecting. But this time, I saw myself in the mirror hovering above my bed. Up, up I went and into the attic of my rental home in Culver City, CA. After admiring the abundance of cobwebs within, I suddenly found myself in a grove facing what looked like a nice juniper tree. However, I soon realized things weren't "normal" per se—the leaves of the tree shimmered in radiant pastel colors.

In a daze, I left the grove and realized I was on the steps of a stone temple. I was still just "winging" it as I decided to go in any odd direction and simply start walking. I went through a thicket, crossing through the bushes. I remember the feeling of pieces of wood and twigs snapping against me. I found a road and followed it for a ways. Looking like a fish out of water, I caught the attention of two people approaching. A male waved his hand excitedly and said, "Hi, welcome to the afterlife!"

I didn't find his humorous literalism to be that funny. I was wide-eyed as they approached me. They were east-Indian and beautiful like a Bollywood couple. The man wore a golden Hindu male dress and the woman a blue sari.

I quickly realized that even in the astral dimension, you're not immune to panic attacks. Having never had an actual panic attack before, I was further caught off guard when, shortly into our conversation, I found myself on my knees weeping. But why was I weeping during such an amazing experience?

"What if this is all in my head?" I cried out. "How do I know you're really here? What if the afterlife is just some elaborate dream all along?"

"Look," the man said as he stamped his feet and kicked up dirt. "You may not feel you're entirely here, but WE are. As you can see, I'm really, *really* here. The day you get to really experience this world, it will be much realer than what's happening right now. What you're doing now is called *astral projecting.* There are boundaries between our world and the world of dreams that are very hard to understand. To come to this world from yours, you must go through those barriers first."

His parting advice for me was to *"overcome the fear"* that holds me back from more proficiently projecting into their world. In no time at all, my eyes opened and I was back in my little bedroom. I jolted up and grabbed my laptop to start jotting down as much of the experience as I could.

This was only the beginning. What ensued was a steady stream of similar experiences, including contact with entities from the other side who saw me as an instrument for easy contact. During this period I started having astral experiences as many as four, five or six times per week. Typically, it would happen in the early morning. If I'd naturally wake up around 5 AM for the bathroom, once I'd lay back down again and close my eyes, inevitably I'd find myself shooting out of my body.

In 2015 I grabbed my bags and decided to take my laptop business abroad and travel for several months. Living out of hostels I continued to have experiences. In London, I encountered a deceased Englishman wandering the halls of a hostel above an old pub. Furiously, he would try to touch and sexually molest the sleeping patrons (despite his hands going through their sleeping physical forms). I yelled at him to "begone." He ran to my bunk and tried to attack my astral form out of vengeance. However, he posed no threat to me even as I felt his hands wrap around my astral neck. I returned to my body easily.

At other times, I'd learn to sustain my experiences in the near-Earth dimension to spy on people in this Earth plane. I would spy on my roommate (and out-of-body mentor and author) Kensho while I lived in Prague, identifying objective details that could be recounted and verified.

Another time at a hostel in Macedonia I wandered the halls as a "ghost," spying on sleeping guests and noticing details that I could verify upon returning to my body. All of this made for an exciting period of journaling as I further confirmed the enormous reality of the subject.

It was at a bed and breakfast in Istanbul where I experienced my first true contact with a deceased loved one. My grandmother, who passed away in 2012, came into my mind as I partially disconnected from my body. The resultant conversation was hardly different from a normal phone-call. We discussed serious issues affecting my family and my father (her son,) plus general strategies of what to do with my life. She suggested grad schools that I should attend and career options. She was confident that if I attended the Harvard School of Education (a school I had never heard of until I later Googled it) it would lead to a fulfilling career as a teacher. She also scolded me for constantly traveling and staying independent—a path that she felt was too much like a vagabond's to be taken seriously.

Despite my grandmother's sage wisdom, she may have been slightly naïve to the enormous costs associated with American private universities (and especially ivy-league institutions,) nonetheless, I appreciated her advice and was thrilled by our reunion.

Many astral experiences would also occur during "regular" and "uneventful" nights—I'd appear in a virtual replica of the old home at the ranch. It would appear my childhood abode had perfectly recreated itself, and it was a place where I, my brothers, and my parents would frequent during dream states. In the astral state, however, it was possible to appear in full lucid consciousness. I would "wake up" in my bed on that side; hardly different from waking up as I normally do on this side.

With little else to do in the astral house, I'd conduct experiments: Just how real and "physical" is the so-called "non-physical" realm? I would try to cook food or I'd write notes and leave them to be recognized on my next trip. At one point, I opened a cabinet and poured a bunch of garlic salt into my mouth. The sudden gagging caused the experience to immediately end and I decided not to try that again.

Sometimes I'd encounter another living family member (such as my father) in the house but in a dream state. When we are in the astral and we encounter a dreamer, it's like meeting a sleepwalker. They are in the environment and interacting with it, but mumbling to themselves and experiencing all types of inner-world activity (what we'd call hallucinations.) They rarely recognize us.

When Concept Meets Reality

While my forays into this realm have been dedicated, there is always a disconnect that seems to occur between theory, experience, and the rational side of our minds. Despite encountering astral residents and having life-altering, paradigm-changing experiences, there is still a separation from how it affects life on a day-to-day basis. Half asleep wandering through Ross to buy underwear at 10 PM, you don't really think about concepts like your eternal, future existence. Our Earthly lives are still fragmented and far away from these grandiose possibilities.

However, if there is ever a time when that gap is closed, it's when a loved one suddenly dies. This is when you are faced with the sudden, harsh reminder that the topic of death (and what happens after) can affect anyone, at any time. It's a reminder that this isn't a frivolous subject that can be placed on the mental back-burner, but it's something that can (and should) be studied in depth as a way to fully prepare for this inevitability (and save a lot of stress in the meantime.)

This reality came crashing down, hard, when in summer of 2016 the dread of so many years accumulated. With every year, and eventually every month that passed, I knew it was only a matter of time before the train wreck back home in Arizona would come to a head. When my mom was admitted to the hospital for liver failure, I knew my worst fears had been manifested.

It was not an immediate death, but there was a grim period of hospital care where she was barely conscious, and doctors tried to feign optimism; but we knew she wasn't going to leave the hospital. I returned to AZ to visit her, and about a week later she was taken off life support.

Stunned, I coped as anyone could, and reserved time to grieve. My understanding of the afterlife certainly helped, but the experience seemed so disconnected from what I knew, and it hardly helped with the grief. I knew I needed to make some type of contact as the only way to alleviate myself. With the intention placed, just days after her passing I began to have astral experiences in my familiar astral replica home. Now, however, my mom was also there.

My mom passed away in a particularly dark mental state; her death the result of the many years of alcohol and substance abuse. When she crossed over, she appeared unaware of what happened. For her, there was no light, life review or greeting party. In retrospect, I am convinced this is because of her extremely insular, unhappy (low vibratory) state of mind, whereupon she likely pushed helpers and guides away from her. Instead, she appeared in the old family house that I'd visited many times before. She was confused as to how she arrived since the house had long ago been demolished. She didn't understand why the TV couldn't function, and she was furiously angry that she had been taken to the hospital. "It was a horrible experience. They stuck a breathing tube down my throat and it was so painful." I sat with her and realized I couldn't exactly tell her that she died. How do you tell somebody something like that? However, she knew "something" happened. She chalked it up to losing her memory or mind—she thought maybe she was suffering from dementia, or experienced amnesia in the hospital.

In following nights, attempts to introduce the notion that she never made it out of the hospital were met by an interesting phenomenon: she would pass out—suddenly leaning over to one side into unconsciousness, and my experience would end. I surmised that some higher power was shielding her from the information for the sake of preserving her sanity. I stopped trying to break the news to her.

Eventually, she did become aware that she had died. In following astral encounters, her emotions were somewhere between ecstatic, euphoric, and terrified. She, however, maintained her composure well enough to greet me when I'd appear astrally, and even serve me food (sometimes cake or fruit.) She'd tell me pieces of information about her experiences, such as how time seemed to work "differently" and in particular time-keeping ornaments (clocks, etc) mysteriously ceased to function.

However, far beyond her experiences in a new, parallel Earth— she reported an overwhelming sense of guilt. All her problems in life were now coming back to haunt her. From allowing herself to be in an abusive relationship, to never pursuing her career and artistic talents to their full potential. She instead chose to live in an insular world fueled by fear, and now this regret was tainting every aspect of her being.

I noticed an interesting phenomenon as reported by renowned out-of-body explorer Jurgen Ziewe ("Multidimensional Man", "Vistas of Infinity") and others; which is that when I'd see her and she was happy— she had a luminance about her and she looked physically 20 years younger. However, when she was in a dark mood, the luminance was gone and she appeared as old and unhealthy as before she passed. This is the higher-density effects of the afterlife in action. People's minds are directly affecting their environment, projected in a radius around them. Here, if someone is in a bad frequency, you may be able to sense or feel it—but in the afterlife you can actually see it. A person's thoughts may even manipulate matter around them, as negativity automatically corrodes and decays—whether causing one's appearance to age or the green grass to wither and brown.

A couple of weeks passed and I had no experiences. By the next time I was projecting again, things had changed. At some point between my last encounters with my mom, the dark side had overtaken her. A mental breakdown had occurred. I did not appear in the replica home, but I was now in a hospital facility. A middle-aged woman appeared with brown hair tied up in a bun, wearing a nurse's outfit reminiscent of the 1950s style. She brought me to see my mom, but warned me ahead of time that she was in a "dark place." I entered and discovered my mom was in a large private room, lying on a white bed. Her state was dark indeed. She was filled with anger, and I could sense it. To my terror, she was using some of the same hospital equipment that was used on her before her death to mutilate herself. Presumably, she created the equipment through her mind, materializing it through her intense emotions. "Look what they did to me!" she screamed at me as she tortured herself with the instruments; blaming me for what had been an undoubtedly hard week in the ICU before her breathing tube was removed and she died. My mom wanted to die peacefully at home—she was livid that we called an ambulance the day her skin started to turn yellow from jaundice.

This behavior was not new to me. My mom was (and is) bipolar. For all the loving and warm energy she produces, she is capable of an equal amount of darkness. This, however, was too much. Knowing her psychology and how to talk to her, I helped her snap out of this horrible state of mind and I began asking her questions about life in the astral. Thankfully, this briefly took her mind off what she was doing to herself— and a little bit of peace was restored.

"It's hard to find good food here," she complained (she was an avid chef.) "In this world, you don't have to eat to stay alive. As a result, people forget how to cook!" We managed to have an enjoyable visit together, yet she was teetering on the brink of madness. It filled me with great stress and remorse. Eventually I left her room and ended the experience.

I "woke up" distressed and angry. A lifetime of my mom being unable to manage her own problems, and ultimately manifesting them on others came back with a sting. I had a realization that just dealing with her in this state of mind was incredibly painstaking and emotionally draining. Now, she was being taken care of by professionals, in a parallel dimension far away from my father. I didn't need to let the stress of my relationship with her consume my mind anymore. I decided I didn't want to see her again.

My decision, however, only lasted for a couple of months. Eventually, the contacts resumed (perhaps guided by decisions I make in my astral life that I am unaware of on Earth—we all have parallel lives on the other side, but that's another topic.) When I saw my mom again, she was still in the hospital facility. However, this time I came to meet her in a kind of lounge (it was like a log cabin made of red mahogany and was erected across from the primary care facility along the shores of a huge lake.) There were others present, and this time my mom was on a high vibration again (she looked luminous). We discussed more about life on her side.

"I went swimming the other day in a pond," she remarked. "There was no negative elements you'd expect in a regular swimming hole in the woods. It's like it was designed for our own enjoyment." She described beach bonfires, new friends she'd made, and her return to doing art.

Feeling overjoyed to see her becoming healthier, I returned to this side with a greater sense of morale. A couple of weeks later I had an even more stunning encounter. This time, she decided to try to visit me. In a half-asleep state, her voice called out my name as clear as a bell. Wearing a plaid dress, she appeared in my bedroom, crawled up next to me and put her arms around my waist (with her trademark sense of humor, she prefaced the experience by saying "This is going to be really creepy.") As she held me, we chatted for 10 or 15 minutes about various subjects. She talked more about life in her world, that she had acquired a "large pet moth" that lived outside her door in her casita. She noted that in her plane insects lived and died in the soil as nature continues unblemished. She said she found this phenomenon odd and was not what she expected—she did not believe "heaven" would be a tangible world just like ours.

A week or so passed and I received a phone call from my grieving (and mentally troubled in his own ways) father. Ecstatic, he recounted the same experience with my mom visiting him—down to the same outfit. It had occurred on the same morning.

My connection only became stronger when, a couple of weeks later, my appointment with famed medium Susanne Wilson was finally scheduled. This experience could be an entire chapter itself (and I've written about it thusly; Google *Cyrus Kirkpatrick / Susanne Wilson*. An article appeared on suspense novelist Michael Prescott's blog.) In summary, Susanne had no awareness of who I was, and I did not yet publicly post information about the details of these experiences. She, however, was immediately patched through to the nurse I encountered in my first astral experience at the hospital (her name is Mrs. Connor.) Extremely evidential and personal information was brought forward, including a four-way conversation between my mom's caregiver (Mrs. Connor,) myself, my mom, and Susanne herself. Among my mom's questions was if I was able to physically feel her when she wrapped her arms around my waist during my out-of-body experience when she materialized. She explained that she was taught to try to connect physically during such an encounter; as physical touch creates the greatest impact upon a loved one's memory.

As time passed encounters became less frequent; however, she did materialize a couple more times in the next few months. During these visits there was a bit less brightness to her spirit. She again laid on the bed with me and told me now she spends her days "sleeping and praying," which didn't seem particularly positive.

My hunch was right: At some point the hospital facility (it was called the *Halls of Healing*) had discharged her. I warned her that she should get a new life of her own versus returning to the old memories of the replica house.

"No," she countered. "In that house, you appear there when you are sleeping, and I need to be closer to you." I knew, however, that her plan was a bad idea. Not only would the ranch house bring her closer to my father during his astral states—returning her to the dark grips of the same toxic and controlling relationship that led to her physical death, but it would keep her chained to her past.

My mom's visits would continue, up to the present day. While she still visits the replica home, she fortunately did not bind her life to that place and she appears to have a life of her own now that extends to new horizons. In fact, I even appeared once with her in a white villa and she explained we were in Italy (*astral* Italy, of course.) She was with some new boyfriend and described it as a summer vacation. I even sat and watched a movie with her once (we saw *Hail Ceasar* before I watched it in this dimension. It wasn't very good either time, unfortunately.)

Today, she has a greater grip on things. She's still my mom, with many of her continued quirks and eccentricities, and sometimes we've even been known to have quarrels, but that is how our relationship has always been.

And, she continues to visit my father—sometimes appearing in front of him—here in the waking world. In Christmas 2017, she popped in and audibly exclaimed "Merry Christmas!" before phasing back out. Around the same time, she also started coming into my room and shortly before I'd greet her in the out-of-body state, she'd interact with the environment—such as flipping the switch of my heater on or moving something from a shelf to get my attention. When I know she's in my room, I can focus on leaving my body and I'll know she'll be on the other side to see me.

More Join Her Side

In summer of 2017 one of my brothers named Jason—long the rock of the family and a stable, larger-than-life personality—suddenly and unexpectedly died of pancreatitis.

Much like my mom, it turned out his death was almost entirely attributable to abuse of alcohol, pills and other substances that exacerbated a pancreatic condition.

It felt like only yesterday I was joined by all my brothers as we went to scatter our mom's ashes. Now, suddenly, one of our own was gone and it would be his turn to be scattered. As he was shrouded by skepticism and religious fundamentalism I never got to tell him about any of my astral experiences—nor the communication with our mom. This made me worried that his death would have been more fearful than necessary.

My fears were amplified when I went to visit my mom in the OOB state, and she explained that despite her son's crossing she still hadn't heard from him nor seen him. What could that mean? What realm did my brother find himself in? It was a terrifying thought, and we were both uncertain about the situation.

Later on, I experienced something closer to a dream-state than an astral state. In that dream, I was being shown my brother. He wore a long grey cloak with a hood as he wandered the near-Earth plane; acting essentially as a voyeur but fulfilling various curiosities as he went to see things he'd never gotten to see while in his Earth body.

By my next (true) astral experience, I briefly "woke up" to find myself in the basement of a house. Music was playing and my brother and my mom greeted me—it would appear they were having a party together. They tried to give me a little 100-page booklet by an African author related to an explanation of what "really" happens when we cross over from the Earth plane. I think even in their world they are a bit unaware that I actually write books about such topics in my realm, and I didn't need the education! I tried to "hang on" but like happens so often in these experiences, my consciousness started spiraling downward and the experience faded.

In a more recent lucid conversation with my mom, I asked about my brother and she said, "Jason's fine. Don't worry about him. I was with him yesterday."

Expanding the Astral Experiences

The experiences with my mother were the most personal and powerful encounters with the other side. They also revealed, beyond the shadow of a doubt, that we can continue relationships with people who have crossed over. Far from being dead, the numerous visits and conversations with my mom (and now my brother) in the months following her death were more detailed than any we had on this plane for years. Since her death, our relationship has improved. In fact, even my relationship with my grandmother during our one twenty-minute "phone call" was the best conversation I'd had with her since perhaps I was a child.

As a side-note, my grandmother has also been highly active with my father, appearing sometimes along with my mother and my aunt, all in a drawn-out attempt to help him overcome his mental crises. It's been a joint effort between the three of us to help my father in this regard. So not only are these family members still in my life, we actively work on projects together.

Becoming talented at astral experiences also expands far beyond just seeing loved ones. I've had some other extremely notable encounters that further broadens my imagination about what might be possible.

In late 2016, at some point in between visiting my mom, I had a most unusual experience: As often occurs with a projection trip, it began as a lucid dream, but then I collapsed the dream imagery (the dream imagery is a kind of holographic field the mind projects,) and found that I was in a real environment. As often happens, I am temporarily flooded by memories of my second-life in the astral (sadly, these memories are barely retained,) and I "knew" I was in the astral equivalent of Arizona, where I had been out with friends in the city (it could have been Tucson or Phoenix, I am unsure.) I was on the steps of a bar. This, however, was a most unusual bar. Titled the "Punch You, Punch Me Bar and Grill" it was a venue dedicated to MMA enthusiasts.

Inside, men with large, fashionable beards punched, fought and put each other in headlocks. It was raucous and there was more than an ample amount of alcohol being passed around.

Finding the place quite bizarre, I looked around to get more information. I went to the bar and encountered a young man with a winning smile (an "All American" type of guy, maybe in his early twenties.)

He explained that the bar was a place for people who love MMA to fight each other without consequences. Of course, in the astral, there's no fear of long-term wounds or disabilities—people can practice martial arts on each other to their heart's content.

So, I partook, fought a guy with a large beard, and promptly lost. Big surprise.

I returned to the bar and chatted up the bartender again. I told him I was astral projecting which meant I only had a few minutes left, tops, before my experience would end—so I'd like all the information I could, and that I wanted to know his story.

He told me that in life, he was first getting into sports activities, in particular MMA fighting. He discovered how much he loved that type of thing; however, "BAM, one day I dropped dead of a heart attack. The day after I was finally recognized in athletics. So here I am now, continuing what I love on this side."

An idea popped into my head. "Please, tell me your full name. This experience is about to end, but I want to see if I can look you up."

"Hmm, okay," the man replied. "My name is John Doe." His name is not John Doe, but to protect him and his family, we'll use this name.

The real name he provided was fairly unique. So, I was excited about what would happen after I put it into Google. Almost immediately I saw the same face I encountered in the projection experience. It was his Facebook memorial page.

Only several months prior, a young man tragically died in the Phoenix, AZ area. With his whole life ahead of him, his death occurred only a couple of days following his earning a medal for obtaining first place in a local athletic competition. He was a celebrated tech-genius and considered extremely talented by his employers. He was only nineteen-years-old.

There was information present, however, that this young man failed to tell me: It was not a heart attack that caused his death. Rather, he took his own life.

What followed was an internal debate: the ethics of contacting the young man's family to share the experience. I discussed the situation at length on my Facebook community ("Afterlife Topics and Metaphysics") and finally decided I'd send a message—even if I were thought of as a predatory monster making up encounters with someone's deceased family member, if it brought some type of comfort it may be worth it.

And so, I carefully worded a message to the memorial account. I explained that I had encountered someone in a "dream" who told me his full name, and that after I looked him up it was his same face. I explained I lived in Los Angeles, worked in media and writing, and I was not a psychic nor trying to get anything; but I just wanted to share the experience.

The young man's mother responded. Tragically, she explained that they'd been solicited by countless heartless fake psychics and mediums trying to pinch money out of them. She said she required caution accepting any message like mine, but was giving me the benefit of the doubt, and that despite the fact she was a non-believer in "any and all things" supernatural—she told me a part of her wanted to believe I really encountered her son. She said it was nice to think, if only in theory, that someone else could have possibly experienced her son's undeniable charm and trademark personality—and that perhaps the personality still lives on.

I consulted with a friend and mentor ("Kensho" the out-of-body explorer) about the experience, as he's had many objective encounters like this, as well. He explained to me that I had made a "terrible mistake" by contacting his family—that such decisions, even if they're well-intentioned, generally cause harm to people. However, in the end, I felt I did the right thing.

Almost a year later, an incredible event occurred to place a capstone on this experience: I was invited to be interviewed by the group *Helping Parents Heal*, an organization assisting with grief among parents who lose their children. This same mother had coincidentally joined this group, watched my webinar, and reached out to me again.

She explained that after I contacted her, she decided to find a credible medium. In my original message, I explained how the young man I met worked as a bartender. The medium, with zero knowledge of what I told her, explained how her son had surprisingly transitioned from his life in this world as a computer programmer to instead work *in the hospitality field* in a realm similar to our own; as it allowed him greater social experiences and fun that perhaps he hadn't enjoyed as frequently in his old life.

This, she explained, confirmed what had previously been a far-fetched tale. It also confirmed for me that my experience with her son was entirely real; with details verified through a third-party. It demonstrates the great potential of astral projection as a tool of making contact not only with our own loved ones, but also to relay messages from others we meet.

The Second Earth

These discoveries, such as exploring the astral equivalents of my home cities in Arizona, blended with a greater understanding as I came to realize that there is a vast astral realm that I call *"The Second Earth,"* where many millions of the departed go. And yes, while many of us enter more heavenly realms, many more prefer a continuation of our human lives. And just as our civilization advances with technology—cars, computers, mass communication—so this realm advances alongside us as an astral replica of our own Earth—complete with versions of every major city, and every important geographic territory—from the grimy streets of the astral Bangkok, to countless creative types inhabiting the astral version of Los Angeles—a realm I have also explored (in the hills of astral Hollywood you'll find mansions populated by many great celebrities who long passed on—from Rita Hayworth to Clark Gable.)

This, in itself, presents a type of philosophical rabbit-hole: Is an earthly condition necessary for our soul's growth and development? Although I am a researcher, not a philosopher, I would argue "yes." There is an inherent conflict in a physical (or even pseudo-physical realm) between man and environment. Although more heavenly realms would mean a release from such constraints, and perhaps greater freedom of mobility, thought and expression—the very act of restriction in a physical sphere is required to test the capabilities of the human spirit. That, and of course, there is simply the matter of what a human soul is used to or desires. While perhaps all of us will move toward existences greater than our human forms, we progress along this path at our own level of free will and desire. I believe we advance to other types of realms based on preference and individual growth. No one is coerced into an Earth-like realm; and at the same time, no one is forced to enter a grandiose existence as a being of light. **In summary, the afterlife is not one-size-fits-all. There are both physical realms like ours, and mental "higher" realms, plus millions of gradients in between.**

And, as great astral explorers like Jurgen Ziewe have reported: we do not merely discard our human forms—but they are slowly rarified in form and beauty, until our appearances become "angelic"—or beautiful beyond comprehension, as Jurgen has reported in some of the much higher realms.

However, to arrive at such levels that so many desire is not instantaneous for most souls (unless they were already so highly developed before their Earthly incarnation,) and it requires a long period of progression, including working out our flaws and psychological issues down in the Earthly domains of not only the world we exist in now; but also the amidst the civilizations of the Second Earth—or the countless billions of other inhabited planets across the vast astral universe.

This was demonstrated by my mom's experiences. She did not ascend immediately into a heavenly angelic form at death; rather, she carried with her the exact state of mind before she crossed over. It was through the help of various therapists, as well as myself, that she pulled herself together and rekindled her true potential. This is the nature of how all souls progress.

And so, the Second Earth has become a conceptual afterlife that is far easier for me to wrap my mind around. No longer do I have to struggle to deal with ideas of an afterlife beyond my mortal comprehension; but I can consider elements of lifestyle as they exist now: parties and celebrations, concerts and music, friends and work, careers and hobbies, and even difficulties or challenges as they relate to potentially tough jobs like rehabilitation and / or psychiatric care. Who says the afterlife needs to be "eternal rest"?

Looking Forward to the Future

Personal astral projection and communicating with those who have passed on is only one area of afterlife evidence. As we speak, researchers like Gary Schwartz, R. Craig Hogan, Sonia Rinaldi and others are trying to perfect technology to allow easier communication between our world and higher-density planes. This means the future holds many wondrous possibilities. However, until that time comes, it's critical that we tune our own psychic senses; that we practice astral states, and always seek to reach out to those who have crossed over. Our civilization faces a terribly imbalanced amount of grief, suffering and darkness caused by the death process. We must reinforce our understanding and communications with the other side if we hope to overcome this unbelievable obstacle.

There may come a time in the future when the realities of higher density planes are completely normal. Perhaps there will be embassies to handle communication and relations with such realms, just as there are for foreign countries. Perhaps the idea of a Second Earth to match our own will become part of our regular vocabulary. Until this day arrives we must endure continued hardship and confusion about the nature of life and death.

About Cyrus

Cyrus Kirkpatrick is an afterlife / paranormal researcher and author of the 2015 book *Understanding Life After Death*—and is currently writing a follow-up set to be released in the near future. He is an avid traveler who maintains a travel blog at www.cyruskirkpatrick.com and enjoys going to obscure (sometimes crazy) destinations. His afterlife-related site is www.afterlifetopics.com, and he runs the large afterlife discussion group on Facebook also called Afterlife Topics and Metaphysics. He currently lives in Los Angeles, CA where he works part-time in corporate auto-marketing and full-time as a contractual writer and literary editor for self-published authors. In 2017 he was a featured speaker at the Afterlife Research and Educational Symposium in Scottsdale, AZ.

Add me on Facebook and say hello!

I Choose Love

Scarlett Lewis

Hello, my name is Scarlett Lewis and I would like to tell you how the next chapter of my life unfolded. The morning began like any other. A single mom of two boys, Jesse 6 and JT 12-years-old. My older son, JT, took an early bus first. After he left I would go into Jesse's room and snuggle with him, kissing him until he awoke. Then we would rough house with each other on the bed, tickling and doing acrobatics until it was time to get dressed and out the door. I dropped Jesse off at a daycare centre every morning before going to work.

December 14, 2012 was like any other day. When I arrived at work, I made my round of hellos and then sat down at my desk to go over my day's schedule. One of my co-workers instant messaged me from home and asked if I was watching the news. "There's been a shooting at a school in Newtown," she messaged.

That's terrible, I thought. But then again, nothing can ever happen to your child. Then people began approaching my desk with more news. It was actually a school in Sandy Hook, my son's school! A teacher had been shot in the foot. I thought perhaps it was a jealous boyfriend, but I decided to go to the school to see for myself what was happening.

On my way, friends continued to message me and told me they heard parents were supposed to pick their kids up from a firehouse located at the end of the cul-de-sac where the school was located. All children had been evacuated from the school. My commute was 45 minutes so by the time I reached the school, I had to park 1/2 a mile away. As I came closer,

I began to sense the commotion as helicopters flew overhead while first responders and the military ran about with AK-47's drawn.

By the time I arrived at the firehouse, most of the children had already been picked up by their parents. I scanned the field of children, watching as parents tearfully reunited with them and whisked them away into waiting cars. I didn't see Jesse.

I approached someone in uniform. "Have you seen my son, Jesse?" I asked. He pointed into the firehouse and said, "If you can't find your loved one, we are asking that you go to the backroom and put their name down on a piece of paper."

There's no way I'm doing that, I thought. I'm just going to find my son and take him home, I will just go to the school myself. I walked up the road a bit that was barricaded with wooden blockades and uniformed military personnel. "I need to go to the school to get my son," I said resolutely to one of the uniformed men. In hindsight, I knew at that moment, looking into his eyes, my son was gone. But I swept that thought away as fast as the awareness had come. He motioned for me to go back to the firehouse.

At that point the educators who had come from the school had congregated in the firehouse and were sitting around a table eating pizza. I walked up to them and said, "What happened? Did any of you see Jesse?" I saw a momentary glance between the art teacher and another teacher and she shook her head as if to say, don't say anything. I walked away annoyed. Fine, I will figure it out myself!

I asked someone official looking and they said, "We're sweeping and re-sweeping the school. We believe there are children hiding and it is taking us a while to find them." Of course, I thought Jesse had taken a contingent of kids and hid them somewhere! I found myself, however, entering into the back room that I had not wanted to go into. I discovered the folding table where the list was being kept. It was a piece of lined paper torn from a notebook. There was a long list of names, in fact I had to turn the paper over and put Jesse's name on the backside. Never did I think for one second that all those people were dead.

Right about this time JT texted me, "Mom can I come and wait with you?" The other schools were in lockdown and I told him he could. Of course, because when they find Jesse, he will want to be with his big brother. Maybe we will go out to dinner were my thoughts. My mom, who lives across town, and step-father, came walking up—weaving in and around the vast media who had gathered in front of the firehouse. They had coffee and JT was lagging behind. "Your brothers are coming as well," my mom proclaimed.

"Oh no!" I responded, "Why? They shouldn't leave work for this, it's not a big deal?"

The updates we received throughout the day were vague details of the search being carried out in the school and surrounding areas. There was a rumour that Jesse and a contingent of kids had run to the neighbour's house just to the left of the firehouse. I knocked on the door and asked the older man that answered if he had seen Jesse that morning. He replied that he thought he had but that the kids had been taken to the daycare centered on the other side of the fire station. Neil (Jesse's father) and I were texting. He checked the daycare, no Jesse. "Call the hospitals," I admonished.

"I can't get through," he texted.

"Then go there!" I demanded. And he did. No Jesse.

An officer approached me while we waited and asked me if I had a recent photo of Jesse. He asked me if I remembered what Jesse was wearing. Later, another officer asked if Jesse had any identifying marks on his body.

JT became upset. "What if Jesse isn't coming back," he sobbed. A lightning bolt of strength entered my body at that point and I heard myself, as if in third person, saying, "If Jesse isn't coming back, we know exactly where he is. He is in paradise. We will have a harder time but we will get through it and we will be ok." I wondered where that response had come from and felt a profound gratitude for my faith.

Parents were demanding to know where their children were. The scene was chaotic with reporters pushing to get past barricades in front of the firehouse and first responders trying to contain the situation. Finally, a man walked up to me brusquely, knelt down quickly and said to me in a monosyllabic tone, "There's no easy way to say this, your son is dead."

I wasn't shocked because at this point, a slow understanding was dawning on all of us. He quickly got up and walked away. Two police officers rushed over to me and asked me what he said.

"He just told me Jesse is dead," I responded.

"He wasn't supposed to say that!" They rushed over and apprehended him. But I knew what he had told me was true.

Two of my brothers and their wives had come to wait with us. After we received the news, albeit awkwardly, my other brother arrived with his wife from Boston. I was sitting with JT as I watched my mom walk up to him and give him the news with her hand on his shoulder. His knees buckled as if he had been punched in the stomach. That's when it hit me, as well. My beautiful little 6-year-old son Jesse had been murdered by a former student at Sandy Hook Elementary school, two weeks before Christmas.

I went back to my mother's house who lived across town and we tried to process our loss. We prayed. We fielded calls and started sharing the news with those closest to us. Mostly we sat in shocked silence. I had the realisation that I had to be JT's role-model through this experience. I knew he would be watching my every move, listening to every response. I knew as the head of the family I would have to carefully and thoughtfully navigate our way through this tragedy. I tried to be strong.

The first time I cried was when I read the headlines the next morning and realised the extent of what had happened. I opened a text message sent to me overnight from Jesse's father. Twenty seven people had been massacred that day, including 20 first graders in two classrooms and 6 educators. The young shooter shot his mom while she was sleeping before he came to the school and ended up taking his own life when he heard the police approach. This was one of the worst mass shootings in the history of the United States. I dropped the phone and began to wail.

We found out a short while later from the police investigation that Jesse's brave actions had resulted in saving the lives of 9 of his classmates. When the shooter entered Jesse's classroom he continued his shooting spree, most likely killing his teacher before his gun ran out of bullets. During the short delay and while he was changing his ammunition clip, Jesse called to his friends to run and they followed his command and ran from the room. When the shooter reloaded he killed everyone remaining, including Jesse who we believe chose to stay by the side of his beloved slain teacher.

I think about how in that moment, the school was a war zone. The shooter had a semi-automatic rapid fire weapon and everyone was scattered and scared. And yet, Jesse was able to do what he did, to stand his ground, and die facing the shooter. Keep in mind that what happens to the brain in a fight or flight mode is that it cuts off your reasoning to ensure you simply run. For Jesse to be thinking logically at that point, and standing his ground and calling for his friends to run, gives me comfort because it means he was able to overcome his fear, even to the point that he could perform the ultimate act of courage—which is to lay down your life for your friends.

The following day I made myself a cup of tea and stood for a while at my mom's kitchen sink, looking out at a bird feeder she had put up so she and Jesse could watch the birds feed. I realised then that Adam Lanza had murdered Jesse but that he hadn't murdered JT and I. I was determined that we would be OK, we would turn the tragedy into something to help make the world a better place, and that we would feel joy again. I knew if Jesse could be so courageous, in the face of unmitigated terror, then I could certainly honour his life by living my own and being a part of the solution to the issues that caused the tragedy in the first place.

Later on, I found myself sitting quietly on my mother's couch. I never took time to sit still as a single mom with a full time job. I marveled at how for the first time in my life, seemingly I had no desire to go anywhere or do anything. I thought about how horrible I felt. I felt so bad that at times I thought I was going to die myself. I pictured myself dissolving into dirt and I would gingerly pick up my arm, look at the veins beneath the skin on the inside of my wrist just to check if blood was flowing through them. I felt like I was going to die but I didn't care and was almost surprised that I remained living when Jesse was dead.

At a certain point an incredible feeling came over me, an elation. I sensed the dichotomy of what I perceived as the "dark night of my soul" with the seeming lightness of being. It was this incredible feeling of joy. And I thought about this dichotomy: how can I be feeling this joy when I'm feeling such terrible grief. I realized: Oh my gosh for the first time in my life I'm completely devoid of fear. I have no fear, I am not afraid to die. I had experienced every parent's worst nightmare, I was living it and so I have nothing left to be afraid of. It was such a good feeling.

Then I had this life review, all at once I was shown all of the choices I had ever made. This flashback of seemingly every major decision I had ever had, in chronological order, brought me to an understanding that those choices, every job, every relationship, all of my job decisions were made in fear. At the same time I had complete compassion for myself. There was no judgement. I knew that if I had been able to make those choices based in love and not in fear, that it would have not only benefited me, it would have benefited the world. And so then and there I truly made a commitment to myself that I would start basing all my decisions in love.

I was surprised at how fearlessness felt and how much fear impacts us on a daily basis without us even being aware of it! The experience was so powerful that I've woken every morning since then and set the intention to choose love in every choice I make for the day.

Just after Jesse died how we had so many signs from him and it was incredible. One such blessing began after I went to see a healer. The healer told me that I needed to refrain from taking medication and be present. I needed to be really, really focused on the present moment. The healer explained the reasoning; that this was a very sacred time and Jesse was right there with me—very close, and I would be able to feel him and communicate with him. And of course I was desperate for that. So, I took this advice and stayed very present throughout that time and really incredible things started happening to me.

For example, we'd experience unusual phenomena of headlights flickering on and off. On another morning, all of us awakened at 3 AM after having had the same dream. Another incident involved a toy train I had bought Jessie for Christmas. It was still under the Christmas tree, and the night before we had set it up and put the train track around the base of the tree. My brother and my nephew came over (my little nephew was 4 at the time.) When he saw the train, my nephew said, "Train, train!"

And I said, "Oh my gosh take that train, I can't see it, I don't want it here, please take it." My brother said they couldn't take it, and I said, "Please take it, I don't want it, please take it." And so they took it home with them.

The next morning my brother and his wife, still in bed, heard their son talking in the hallway and he was saying, "Oh is this your train, wow this is a really cool train. What, play with it in the bathtub? I can play with it in the bathtub."

Jesse always played with his toys in the bathtub. I think even more than that it's a knowing when something like this happens, my brother and his wife knew that this was a conversation that was happening with Jesse, and they were sitting in the bed listening. And it was really, really nice. It happened a few more times, too.

JT, Jesse's older brother, was 12 at the time of the tragedy. He found a little note Jesse had left him. It was a little piece of paper folded up on his desk. JT found it a few days after Jesse died and he unfolded it and it said: "Have a lot of fun". Which is such a beautiful message from his little brother to a big brother, because if you think about: why we are here is to learn lessons and to be in service and to help one another, but it's also about having fun. We can't lose sight of that fact, and I knew it was such a beautiful message not only to a brother, but also for the world. To remind us to have fun.

In the life I've been living over the past 4 years I sometimes forget, realising that I'm not having fun. It's as if I have a little bird on my shoulder whispering, you're supposed to be having fun. And I go yes, and it's like a lightbulb—it's just like a switch turns on and thus I turn on the smiles. It's a choice and it doesn't matter what I'm doing—if I'm in front of a crowd and I'm talking, I'll have this little moment where the little voice says, you're supposed to be having a lot of fun, and I go, "Oh my gosh." This "switch" totally changes my demeanour. It is a part of nurturing, healing love; and we are here to give and receive love, as it's a need as basic as food and water. All the love and energy that you give out comes back to you, and that is scientifically researched, that (energetically) what you give out you get back.

Because the tragedy was two weeks before Christmas, you can imagine how hard it was for us on Christmas day. This was after I had done all my Christmas shopping and my three brothers were there with their young children. All the little kids were running around the house, not thinking about our tragedy—the kids were only thinking about the fact that it was Christmas and they were having so much fun, but meanwhile JT and I were not. The loss was too near. So I decided we needed to get away and reconnect. As a single mum, we needed to do something to help us in reconnecting as a family of two. And so within 24 hours, I had plane tickets to Orlando, and a hotel room.

That morning we woke up to a huge snow storm. We started driving to one airport, but the flights were changed, so we had to turn around to another airport where the flights were yet again delayed. This happened three more times before we finally got one.

When we finally got on the plane, they gave us a free movie. Everybody was watching the movies on their screens except for me, because my movie appeared on the screen as only static. Then, suddenly, the screen would shift down 20 channels to a song that was playing. It was playing just for me. I grabbed my phone and I wrote down every word in my notes. I knew it was a message for me. Eventually JT looked over and said, "Jesse?"

I said, "I think so."

During the trip I hadn't spoken to very many people, even friends, but I did have one friend who was checking in on me, and she texted me and asked how the flight was after we landed. I said the flight was amazing—that Jesse was all over the flight—he was messing around with the electronics and sending me messages which were beautiful.

She said something that really struck me, she said, "Sometimes spirits linger around to make sure that you are going to be OK." And I immediately knew what I had to do, but I didn't say anything to JT because it was a fun healing trip.

After we got our bags I said to JT, "Can you watch the bags for a minute? I'm going to run to the bathroom." While in the bathroom I started bawling hysterically and said, "Jessie. If you're lingering to see if JT and I are OK, we are going to be fine. I want you to go be with Jesus." It's my belief that we go to heaven and be with Jesus. And I said that's what I wanted him to do. I said, "If you could be in both places at once that would be great, but if you're lingering just to look after us, I don't want you to linger here, we're going to be fine, I want you just to go. Go be with Jesus." After my prayer I sprinkled down my face with water and went back out to JT. I didn't say anything to him about my concerns, I didn't want to bring him down. I wanted this to be a fun trip for us. I was trying to get things back to normal.

We rented a car and drove out of the Orlando airport, and as we made a right onto the highway, there in the sky, a skywriter was filling the sky with a message that said, Jessie and Jesus together forever. I pull over and we both sat there looking up, not saying anything. I took my phone out to take pictures. Jesse always wrote his name with a backwards J. It felt like he was saying, my mum can be a little slow sometimes, so she doesn't think it's another Jessie I'm going to write this with a backwards J. I couldn't believe it, we sat there in silence and I looked over at JT and he looked at me, and he said: "Jesse's with Jesus."

I said, "I know."

I didn't tell him about the prayer in the bathroom, I was just too overwhelmed. But as we sat there by the side of the road, the plane flies over us again and we're looking straight up at it when it starts to write another message. I say to JT we have to stay and see this other message would say and I know it's for us. And he said he knew, and then it starts writing, "U + God =." Which looks more like a message you would see in a Florida sky. And I said we have to stay close to God to be happy, and he said yeah. And then he said, "Now let's go to Disney World."

That was so comforting to me, because I knew that it was an answer to my prayer. No one knew we were in Florida, no one knew I was going to get off that plane and go into a bathroom and say that prayer, then drive out and see that message. That was a direct answer. I interpreted that as Jesse saying: "I am with Jesus and I am here listening to your prayer too, you wanted me to be in both places and I can be." And that really help me a lot.

Choosing Love over Fear

Why does it take a tragedy for everyone to coalesce and come together and to do incredible acts of kindness and for things to change? I know personally it took a tragedy in my life, it took the vicious murder of my son for me to start living my life in service, because I think when you've had such a terrible loss you realise how love is the only way, and you realise it's the reason why we're all here and that's the only way you can live your life. It's a tremendous life lesson that I feel so blessed to have learnt.

4 years ago I didn't know that we're all here just to help each other. I know it now, and I know that living your life in this way is such a beautiful thing. But it took for me a tragedy. Otherwise, I wouldn't be spreading this message of nurturing healing love because I wouldn't have had it, nor would I have stopped living the fear-based life as before. I wouldn't be a person who consciously chooses love in every action. It's not that I always pull this off, I am human afterall, but when possible I try to choose love, because I know that everything boils down to two fundamental elements: fear and love.

If you can acknowledge that we grow through discomfort, my personal tragedy took me through boot-camp in record time.

I returned home to the small farmhouse I shared with my two boys to pick out Jesse's clothes for the funeral. On my way out I noticed a message he had written shortly before he died on our kitchen chalkboard. He had written 3 words, "Nurturing, Healing, Love." I knew those words are not in the vocabulary of a 6-year-old. They were phonetically spelled because Jesse was in first grade and just learning to write. And I knew there was no way they came from that little boy. I knew immediately that it was like a precognitive moment, maybe not consciously but subconsciously a spiritual awareness that he wasn't going to be on earth for very much longer, and I got a lot from that message. I knew that he had a spiritual awareness and that was a message of comfort for us, but I also knew that he was handing me a torch and it was going to be my mission for the rest of my life. I was going to spread that message and I knew I had to get it in schools. I knew I had to get it in front of kids somehow, but I didn't know how.

The interesting thing is when you break down those words, the meaning of those words, nurturing means loving kindness and gratitude, healing literally means forgiveness and love is compassion in action.

When I saw these words, I was struck with the realisation that if Adam Lanza, the shooter, had been able to give, and receive nurturing healing love, that the tragedy would never have happened. This started my journey of forgiveness. I felt compassion for the boy that was in obvious pain and without connection. I knew, too, that Jesse had a spiritual awareness that he wouldn't be with us for much longer and the message was meant as comfort for his family and friends. I also knew that it was inspiration for the world. This was where we had to turn in order for us to survive, and thrive. I knew I would spend the rest of my life spreading this message, to choose love. I call it a formula for choosing love.

We now have the formula that we teach in our enrichment program in schools. It starts with courage, and that's based on Jessie's courage, and then it goes into gratitude. Picture yourself, or picture me having a little son who has been murdered, and I'm in this dark place. This hole that was so deep no one could pull me out of it except for myself. However, this formula that Jesse left on my chalk board is like a rope that I threw down to myself and my first hand-hold would be the courage to feel grateful. So I started feeling grateful for the things I still had in my life, and we have a lot to be grateful for. We live in a beautiful little farmhouse in a quaint area in Connecticut, and we have horses and dogs and chickens and we have family and friends around, and JT and I have each other. There's always something to be grateful for.

So that's the first step. The second step is being able to contemplate forgiveness for yourself and others. This is gratitude and this is forgiveness. It's about pulling yourself out of whatever situation you're in. And that really sticks, since you are able to find meaning in your suffering and help yourself by being in service to others. We help others because we know helping others is healing ourselves.

That's the formula for choosing love. Each one of those values takes courage. And that's how I came to choose love following the tragedy of my son's murder.

During Jesse's funeral I spoke to the congregation. Everyone had been asking us what they could do. Fortunately, there was indeed something people could do. I asked everyone that day to think about what they thought about and to consciously change one angry thought into a loving one. We know that every thought we have impacts us on a cellular level, mentally, psychically and emotionally. We also know through science that each one of us has between 60-80,000 thoughts per day, and research tells us that between 70 and 80% of those thoughts are negative—angry and non-productive. When we understand this it makes us want to be mindful of our thoughts.

This whole tragedy started with an angry thought in Adam Lanza's head. I pictured him as a little boy, having an angry thought without the tools and nurturing environment to handle such a thought. But an angry thought can be changed. At any time this tragedy could have been stopped.

So please, take an angry thought and change it into a loving thought. Just one thought a day. By doing this, you will make yourself feel better, positively impacting your life and those around you, and through the ripple effect you will create a more peaceful, loving and better world. And, oh my gosh, the feedback I got back from that about a week later was wonderful. People were writing from all over saying this simple action being undertaken everyday was changing their lives. People told me how they'd never contemplated before about what they thought about. And when they started paying attention thoughts, they realised it was easy— they never realised before they had control over the thoughts in their minds.

This is such a beautiful simple and powerful movement, this is the "choose love" movement. It's about choosing love over anger, and we can all do it. We have the courage to do it.

This was how the Jesse Lewis Choose Love Movement was born.

One of my really good friends, who had worked for a company for 25 years, was fired from her job. I asked her to start with gratitude, making that list of three things she is grateful for every day. And she did it! I know she was in a really bad place, but she texted me that night with three things she was grateful for. And you know what, that act changes the wiring in your brain. It gives you the energy to be able to contemplate forgiveness for yourself and for others if you have to, and eventually step outside the busy bubble that we're all in. We all have our lives and our friends and our family and jobs, and we're all too busy, and thus it takes courage to step outside that bubble. Even when you think you're going through a hard time. If you could turn from what's going on in your life and look at somebody else's and help them, then this creates a healing effect upon you.

Sometimes it seems counter intuitive but I can tell you it works, because that's how I did it. I looked outside of my own suffering and pain and started living my life with service. And I realise I have to do that. JT, who's now 16, did that, too. As a child he possessed a wider breadth for compassion, and that's how he could heal himself. JT doesn't do therapy. His therapy is being of service to others.

He started an organisation called Newtown Helps Rwanda. Through this organization, he is now helping kids all over the world. He's continued to do this work for years, because he knows helping others is helping himself. A group of orphaned genocide survivors reached out to him via Skype and through an interpreter. They said, "We heard about what happened to your little brother all the way over here in Rwanda, and we wanted to connect with you to let you know that you're going to be OK and you're going to feel joy again."

I thought to myself, "Oh my god!" These people who survived genocide had so much credibility in my eyes. Up until then, we'd sometimes have people tell us things like, time heals all wounds, and you guys are going to be OK. When people say things like that, I look at them and think you have no idea. You have never been through anything like I have! And so, it was an incredible experience when these two orphaned genocide survivors reached out to us. These were kids who survived a travesty far worse than us. But they found a path to healing similar to ours.

When the genocide happened in Rwanda in 1994, over 1 million Tootsie's were murdered by their neighbouring Tutus in 100 days. These victims were children then, and now they're young adults. They shared each of their stories, which were very different. They told JT how they recovered once they arrived at an orphanage, and while their physical wounds were healing. They said we'd recognize the steps toward healing. They said they started feeling a profound sense of gratitude for the little things, for safety and food, and that led them on to find forgiveness for, who they called, the killers. Because if they didn't forgive them, they would be going down the same path of anger and destruction as them. This allowed them to step outside of their own universe of pain and to instead be in service, sharing their story with others; and in that way, they found meaning in the suffering by helping other people.

JT went to school the next day and started raising money for them to go to university. Being orphans, they would never have been anything other than subsistence farmers because they had no running water or electricity or anywhere to live. So JT started an organisation called NewtownHelpsRwanda.org, and started selling little rubber bands you put around your wrist. Within a couple of months, he Skyped back to announce that he had raised enough money to send one of them to university for one year plus, and an additional amount to help her family. He then he made a personal commitment to raise money for the next three years, which by the way he has done—and he is now sending another orphaned genocide survivor to graduate school.

Following the tragedy of Jesse's death, I received condolences from around the world, including a 6 page, handwritten letter from a man whose young son had died ten years prior from a terminal illness. He told me for all those years he was tormented by asking himself the reason why. Why did this happen to my son? Why my family? Why me? Why did it happen in this way? Why did it have to happen now? He concluded his letter to me like this, "Perhaps now I know the reason why. Perhaps it was so that I could write you this letter and tell you not to spend the rest of your life asking why. Because that's what I've done and I realise now, it's not so much the why, but, the why not?"

My grandmother, Nan, used to always say to my mom, "Maureen, quit asking why, it just is!" This advice helped me immensely. This helped me move more quickly to ACCEPTANCE. The acceptance of my reality. A tough reality, but one that I couldn't deny when I returned home that evening without my young son. Resistance to reality adds to our suffering. Railing against "what is" won't ever change it. As Carl Jung pointed out, "What you resist, persists."

Resistance leads to avoidance. Avoidance leads to anxiety, depression, substance abuse and greater suffering. When you resist or avoid, you miss the tremendous learning opportunity that the difficulty presents to you. And you miss the opportunity to be part of the solution. I accepted my situation, still at times with shock and sorrow that something like that happens in our civilised world, and learned my greatest life lessons from my personal tragedy. I am a much stronger and capable person than I was before losing Jesse. And the most important lesson I learned is that we are all just here to help one another.

Everyone just wants to feel good, and choosing love is the best way of doing that. It is your power. As human beings we all want to be loved and want to love. It's what connects us all and what evaporates our perceived differences. It is our choice, and you can teach someone how to choose love.

It's what Jesse left us, the formula of choosing love. This is the basis for the Choose Love Enrichment Program which we are presenting to schools. It's completely free, because it is so vitally important for people to understand they can choose love in their lives.

A lot of what we see around us is lack of love, mostly fear. Can you imagine a world that Jesus loves? That's the world I want to live in.

The School Program

The priority of teaching in most schools is, unfortunately, not the skills and tools you need for a happy and well-adjusted life. Primarily, formal education is focused on academic learning—not the essential knowledge and wisdom needed to be resilient, connected and compassionate. This latter kind of teaching is called Social and Emotional Learning. Even though everyone knows lessons about how to have healthy relationships, how to manage emotions and make responsible decisions, to name a few, are paramount to personal success—we continue to assign more value to remedial academics and test scores.

Working closely with educators, we created the Choose Love Enrichment Program that teaches children and their educators how to choose love for themselves and others. The program leads with the understanding that we can't always choose what happens to us but that we can always choose how we respond and we can always respond with love. We teach how to label and manage emotions, how to connect in positive, healthy ways, resilience and personal responsibility. We included neuroscience and post-traumatic growth research.

The whole program is taught under the umbrella of a profound and powerful formula for choosing love: courage = gratitude + forgiveness + compassion in action = choosing love. It has been downloaded in 47 states and 17 countries, including Australia, in 2017!

163

These tools and skills cultivate the ability to not only bounce back from adversity, but to thrive. If we don't receive social and emotional learning when we are younger, we find ourselves seeking these tools and skills out when life throws us a curve ball and we are suffering. We must be taught these skills, they are not innate. Decades of research shows that learning these 21st century life skills enables us to have deeper meaning in our lives, greater satisfaction, and better perspective.

I invite you to join the movement to choose love. We can't control what others do, but we can control what we think, our feelings and ultimately our behaviour. And we can choose love, the most important choice we make on a daily basis. If you feel called to help us spread this message of Choosing Love, I would love to hear from you.

About Scarlett Lewis

Scarlett Lewis, mother of Jesse Lewis and JT Lewis, founded The Jesse Lewis Choose Love Foundation in honour of Jesse and to spread the message he left on their kitchen chalkboard shortly before he died, Nurturing Healing Love, the formula for choosing love, and to promote social and emotional education in schools as well as a consistent message of compassion in our communities.

Scarlett is the recipient of the International Forgiveness Award, the Live Your Legacy Award and the Common Ground Award for her advocacy work for peace and forgiveness. When she became a parent for the first time, Scarlett wrote and published a children's book, Rose's Foal. Following Jesse's death, Scarlett wrote, "Nurturing Healing Love", a story about her journey of turning personal tragedy into something that can positively impact the world. An artist and avid horsewoman, Scarlett lives on a small horse farm in Connecticut with her son and animals.

Visit her website at   www.jesselewischooselove.org

Love Eternal
A Soul's Journey
Ainsley Threadgold

During the late spring of 1993 I was in the last school term before we would break up for the summer holidays. Due to the memory loss I suffered, I don't recall exactly which month it was – but my life would suddenly change direction, with events that I would have never imagined.

What I do remember is that for some weeks during that time, I became obsessed with what it would be like to break a bone. I would ask different people what it had been like for them and almost become jealous of their experiences. I know it sounds odd – why anyone would be jealous of something like that? Looking back now I feel that I was in the midst of being somehow aware of what was about to transpire, whilst simultaneously creating it, too. My focus was powerfully on the subject of broken bones, I know from the many synchronicities in my life since, that my vibrational output to the universe was helping to create the circumstances that I had predestined.

I am a firm believer that we, as souls, choose the lives that we are about to embark on. We choose the events that will help shape our experiences; we choose who we are going to be and who we are going to experience these things with. I also (as I will explain in this chapter) believe that we are omnipresent beings; we exist in our physical forms but also everywhere and everywhere else all at once. As the only real moment is that of the present moment, to have a 'past' or a 'future' they all have to be moments that exist in their own present states. These states all happen now, so any choice we make using our free will is perfect because it inevitably takes us to the next key moment and the next key person.

During the weeks leading up to my accident I was creating my own path to a predestined event, I just didn't know at the time that this is what I was doing.

One very uneventful day after school (or so I thought), I was to help my father and younger brother deliver leaflets to households in my local area. I grew up in a village, so inevitably some of the houses were 'out in the sticks' and off country lanes where there was limited space to walk or stand safely away from any traffic. The whole evening ran uneventfully and we all piled into the car so that my dad could drive us all to the last location. The last thing I remembered about that journey was seeing the signpost of the lane we turned onto.

For anyone reading this who has had a big operation and who has been placed under general anaesthetic, you will all know what it feels like to be "put under," you get asked to count to ten, and by three you're out. The world goes black for what seems like a few seconds, and then you groggily wake up. This is what my memory was like surrounding the events that would be hidden from me for 21 years.

A number of hours after those last memories, I woke up. I remember feeling at peace, yet where was I? I was in a bed that wasn't my own, in a strange room with a curious orange glow coming from a window behind me. As I looked around I could see my mum, my dad and my brother sitting on plastic chairs lined against the opposite wall. "What happened, where am I?" I asked. The interesting thing was that I wasn't particularly panicked. Looking back now, I realise that as a 13-year-old kid, I should have at least been a little concerned. I had no memory of what had happened and didn't know where I was, the answer though became quickly apparent as I had it explained to me that I had been run over and had broken my leg.

Although I remember most of the events after I woke up, for years afterward my parents would exclaim how confused I was and how poor my short-term memory was during my first few days in the hospital. What was clear was that I was somehow different. The watch I was wearing when I was run over had been broken so I had a new one bought for me as a get well present; the problem was that after a couple of weeks, it stopped working. I thought perhaps the battery was faulty; yet, I had another that stopped working, too. In fact, every watch I had after that time broke.

This wasn't the only thing I noticed. As the years rolled on, I realised that I affected radio signals, mobile phone signals, and CD's would regularly skip where they hadn't before. I also had an increasing urge to know why I was here; I could write a book on different experiences which kept drawing me back to that same question: "Why am I here?"

There have been many painful experiences in my life, many times where I have acted in a manner that had knowingly or unknowingly hurt people – many occasions where I just wanted the earth to open up and take me down into its cold soiled depths. However, despite that, I have emerged knowing that each breath I have taken was perfect, each interaction meaningful, and each choice purposeful.

Every part of my life had played out exactly as it needed to, to lead me to the next experience, the next twist or turn, almost as if I was being guided. I had asked why I was here and I wanted to know what for, I wanted the void in my memory to hold some meaning, perhaps from which I could make some sort of sense out of the mire I felt I was in. This would reveal itself in ways that I could never have imagined.

At the end of 2011, I signed the dotted line on a contract for a job that I had wanted since I was 14 – I had finally secured a position as a police officer. This, it seemed, came with a rather drastic catch; I would have to do my initial 6 months training in London, which meant living away from home. The other catch was that I would have to agree to take my first posting in the city of Nottingham which was over 70 miles away from where I lived. Without going into too many details, I was at the cusp of a rather nasty breakdown. This manifested in numerous ways, such as how, on a number of occasions, I fell asleep at the wheel of my car whilst driving home. Overall, it was as if I was dying inside. I was also playing my part in slowly ending my marriage. Suffice to say; the next few years would take me on a journey that would create the backdrop to my current story – it would be the night sky to the stars that now shine so brightly across it.

By the summer of 2014, although my then wife was pregnant with our daughter, I was physically, emotionally and spiritually in the worst place of my life – life's events had taken their toll, and something had to change. However, as they say, "The night is darkest just before the dawn." I was off work because of developing acute sciatica, and the sciatica had affected exactly the same part of my leg that I had broken over 20 years earlier. This rekindled a yearning within me, a yearning to know what had actually happened: Why had I still maintained a huge black hole where my memories should have been?

This question would draw me to see an osteopath. During one of the sessions, I asked him whether there was a relationship between where the sciatica had affected my leg and where I had originally broken it, and I found myself telling him about the blank in my memories and all the after affects, too. It was then that he gave me a book on NDE's by Dr Penny Sartori. He told me that he himself had experienced an NDE, and it sounded like I could have had one too – I just didn't remember it.

That was the moment – the moment when everything started to change, where the first break of dawn was creeping over the horizon of my life. It was the first time that I started to feel synchronicities weave their way through my life as I was living it. After devouring the book, I could see a really strong link to my experiences and those of the NDE accounts. I still didn't have any memories but I had a place to start. There was an email address on the back of the book for a UK based support group, so I sent my query to them – I wanted to know if they were aware of anyone else that had experienced an NDE yet carried no memory of it.

A week went by and I hadn't heard anything, so me being me, I started to do my own research. I was suddenly given a flash of inspiration – I kept asking myself, "How am I going to tap into those lost memories?" Then it came to me. Hypnotherapy, of course. It all made perfect sense suddenly – perhaps through hypnotherapy I could tap into those lost memories. In fact, it didn't matter whether I would recover memories of an NDE or whether I would have to relive being run over, I now just needed to know what happened. I was ready to heal from the 20 year-old mental scars.

After doing some research, I found two people in my area who were qualified as clinical regression hypnotherapists. I looked at both the adverts but was only drawn to one, I couldn't explain it at the time but something deep within me felt right. Feeling like I had been guided, I followed my instincts and called a lady named Karen. We spoke on the phone for over an hour. Her genuine enthusiasm shone through and I booked an appointment for the following week. On the day of the appointment I went in with an open mind – I was now ready to face reliving the accident that had caused me so much pain. I knew that whatever I discovered, it would lead to a great healing.

Karen spoke to me of the process and ensured that I knew what was going to happen. I felt safe knowing that she would be the perfect guide. As the process started, Karen got me to visualise relaxing, and then she took me further into myself and into my mind's eye. I was led to a path with a series of doors to my right. I was asked to choose the door which felt right; then when I was ready I could step through.

Once through, Karen got me to describe who I felt I was, what I was wearing and where I was in time. Fully through the door, I found myself on the floor half buried in a ditch at the roadside. I could feel that I was 13 and that I had been run over – I was back at my accident. Dazed and confused, I became increasingly upset. I just wanted my mum and I couldn't get up, why couldn't I get up? I then felt being put into the ambulance. Whilst in there, I felt a presence next to me; it was my mum's dad, Tom. He had died 3 months before I was born, but was now with me. He held my hand and comforted me, telling me how brave I was. He also wished for me to tell my mum that he was so proud of her. He then told me to close my eyes.

After my granddad Tom whispered the melody of his comforting last words to me, I closed my eyes and drifted away. My next conscious thoughts were of floating in a bright space above the clouds. As I became aware of my environment, I also became aware that I was being drawn forward – it was as if I was floating in a river and the gentle currents were guiding me along its course. On looking around I saw a figure dressed in white robes, he was moving towards me and me to him. When I was close enough, I became aware of standing rather than floating. The man knelt in front of me, placing one hand on my chest and the other on my cheek, and he spoke in the most loving tones, "Hello child, I am the Carpenter, you know me as I know and love you, as I know and love everyone. You are a very special boy and I have a job for you to do: I want you to speak for me, I want to speak through you." His words came through my heart, almost like he was communicating with emotion. It was the purest love I have ever felt. He then guided me to understanding that I would be sent back, but in "more favourable circumstances than those of which I left." Being hit by the car had killed me, the child's body that I left was too broken for me to return and live life as I needed to, to do the work I had chosen to do from the beginning.

I now know that part of the reason why I had my experience was for me to accept the gift of my soul's choices, all of them, for every divine twist and turn would come to fruition.

As the Carpenter knelt in front of me, he continued to guide me to understand that part of the original circumstances of my accident would be overwritten, that going back would mean not only being different, but entering into a physically different body; for the injuries would be changed into injuries that I could heal from, to those that would allow me to function normally – and I would be given the experience with my granddad Tom as a key to the memories of the child that died. The Ainsley that was run over and killed is not quite the same Ainsley who is writing these words.

On understanding this, the Carpenter gave me a ball of energy and told me that I could choose to go back, or to stay – my choice would be perfect either way. I was shown all the "me's" that had existed at the same time, and I knew suddenly that we are all omnipresent beings and that time was an illusion. In fact, we actually exist outside of time. We are all the choices made and unmade. I was shown that all the other me's that had been brought to this point had decided to stay; they had held the ball of energy, felt everything and decided that it was too much. As I allowed the ball to speak to me, I felt as if all its knowledge was downloaded to me, almost like an energetic data transfer. I could feel all my Karma from many lifetimes, all the issues that I had carried forward life time after life time, unresolved hurts, traumas, everything. I also experienced the life I would live if I chose to go back. I knew in that moment that I would have to live for many years without any memory of my experience but I would be affected by it. I saw, felt, smelt, tasted and experienced all the unconscious suffering I would cause. I felt all the tears I would not be able to shed, tears that I would cause others to shed for me.

In those moments I knew that I would have to play a part, be a shadow of my potential, the shadow to my light. I would have to live a life of contrast before I could start to shine. In that moment, I didn't want all that, it was too much, in that moment I was both a being of light and the 13-year-old, I was scared: why , why go back to cause all that hurt, to be so closed off from myself and from others? It was the choice I couldn't see beyond. I wasn't shown my potential, or what good I would do after those years in the barren dessert of my empty mind. I was just told that I had a job to do and that I would be spoken through. Where were my guarantees? Why couldn't I also get a vivid picture or download of what my purpose would be?

None of this seemed fair at all. The child in me 'stood' holding the ball and just wanted to give it back. Then something happened, something changed the scenario. Something I hadn't expected which made all of what I had experienced feel worthwhile. The Carpenter stood up and moved away, and then, another figure replaced him. Now a woman was stood in front of me. She was Beautiful, simply, purely, sublimely beautiful, her smile was like sunshine, her voice like the breeze dancing on top of a warm ocean wave, caressing my inner being as it lapped on my shore. She knelt as the Carpenter had and very gently held my face. "Hello my love, you don't know me yet, but you will, we have work to do you and I, when the time is right come and find me."

Man . . . Those words, that voice. It sang to the centre of me. The centre of my centre. It was like being able to taste sunlight and embrace the stars. Who was she, why did I just know her; I had never met her in my earthly life, so why did I feel like we'd been together for an eternity? She looked like an angel yet I knew her in human form.

I was given some space to decide with my heart, and suddenly I was sat on some moss covered rocks by the ocean on a warm summer's day. I suddenly understood that love was an ocean – that I should never be afraid of it drawing back, because it would always wash over me again. That the drawing back, would be likened to me loving myself and peeling back the layers of karmic pain. I would need to clear that pain if I chose to go back.

My heart was set and my soul was made up. I would go back. I would live carrying the weight of all that I needed to be, so that at exactly the right times I would start to remember and become who I really am. That I would journey blind, so one day I could help others see and I'd finally get to meet her – the angel lady who asked me to come find her. I'd finally know who she was to me and who I was to her.

The recovery of these memories has taken nearly 3 years. The initial memories were unlocked by the hypnosis, I didn't realise at the time but there were more memories to be brought forth. It is through hindsight that I now fully understand why I didn't recover the whole experience (as I have written it here) until the right time. Just like with my carrying amnesia of those events after my accident – I was to recover the experience in pieces as it suited my predestined path. I have had 3 occasions since 2014 during deep meditation where I have been brought back to that sacred place in the sky, where I have been nourished with another course in the sublime meal of my experiences on the other side.

After I'd had my initial hypnotherapy session I was contacted by the NDEUK group that I had e-mailed a few weeks earlier. It felt right to share my initial experiences with them. In my recall at the time I only remembered meeting the Carpenter and of him telling me that he was going to speak through me, and this was enough to set me on my path. The group were very helpful and grateful for my sharing, and this in turn rekindled a spark in me that I had not felt in years: not since during my mid 20's (in 2005) when I was guided to Christianity. At that time, a little like I was 2014 – I had come to a very low point in my life, I was in a lot of debt (that I had hidden) and I felt the weight of everything and it was too much to bear.

After finally admitting my money issues and feeling the loving embrace of forgiveness, I felt for a short time that I had found a sense of purpose. I quickly developed spiritual gifts such as praying in tongues and ministry, I also found that I could interpret messages when others were praying in tongues.

Looking back, I can see that my being in church at that time helped me develop gifts that I wouldn't fully understand until the Carpenter told me that he would speak through me. There were countless occasions where I would speak and feel a power behind my words, like my throat was on fire. It always felt like I was channeling. That initial awakening would quickly guide me away from the church setting. During a prayer session I heard a voice speak to me, "Ainsley open the box." I then felt God's presence with me. I was guided by images of God being uncontainable, and my being in church was narrowing my perspective; I was boxing in God because I thought I should. It came at a time when my own perspectives and some of the concepts being taught in church weren't marrying up.

I then found the first "Conversations with God" book by Neale Donald Walsh, and his words made so much more sense to me. For a time after, I felt closer to my true self. Like with the waves of the ocean though, what flooded my beach was to lovingly withdraw. It wasn't quite time for me, there was more contrast that I would have to experience, although I didn't know it at the time my soul had chosen a particularly beautiful path for me.

The reintegration of my yearning to serve (after recovering my memories) reminded me of how good it felt to want to help others. I knew that we are all divinely loved and I wanted to help in any way I could, so I offered my services to the group which was being run from London. Due to an increasing interest in the NDE phenomenon, they were getting flooded with requests for support and information – so much so that they wanted to open a similar site closer to where I lived. I was asked if I would like to assist. Of course, I was more than willing to help out where I could. I had been gifted with memories of my inward journey to heaven and I couldn't think of anything more beautiful than to be able to give back.

This was to form part of the biggest changes in my life. I was introduced to a lady called Kelly – she had also had a NDE a few years earlier and had been told that like-minded souls would unite and come together to collaborate and help affect change across the planet. On speaking to Kelly I quickly found out that she had met Dr Penny Sartori, who had written the book that led me so beautifully to recovering my experience.

In January 2015 Kelly convinced me to join Facebook, she told me that there were a number of wonderful NDE groups that were very open and supportive. Initially I found this to be true, however by the middle of March both Kelly and I were subjected to abuse from one of the groups. After we both left, Kelly told me that she wanted to create a page called The Positivity Power Movement. I thought it was a wonderful idea and offered to help wherever I could. The group quickly took off and it appeared that likeminded souls were coming together.

One of the wonderful if not challenging experiences during this time was to create video posts. We were challenged to talk from the heart about what we felt we wanted to do to serve others. One of my videos was inspired by a picture post of a little girl – she had her hands raised in the air because she thought the cameraman was holding a gun and was going to shoot her.

Being moved by this, I spoke from a very deep and passionate place about our frailties and how like acorns we could grow into oak trees. Little did I know that this video would have a greater impact than I could have anticipated. Someone had viewed my video post several times and was drawn to me for reasons she could not fathom.

Krista lived in the US but had happened upon Penny Sartori's work, and they had swapped some emails and Penny introduced Krista to Kelly, Kelly invited Krista to the Positivity page whereupon she viewed my video post. A while after we initially started to communicate, Krista told me that my post had hit her like an express train. Little did either of us know where our interactions would take us. All we knew at the time was that our interactions were always divinely charged and that we were meant to do something special together. We know now that the universe had divined a plan so beautifully ingenious that we couldn't help but find each other – our stories had written themselves into each other, and now we found ourselves inseparable.

Although our lives couldn't be more different or further apart, love found a way of helping us find each other, then helping and continuing to help our love grow. It grew through my painful insecurities and through our ego's need to run away and hide. It gave us such an incredible strength that even the 6,000-mile gap between us and the 5-hour time difference couldn't keep us apart. We were both at the end of relationships that had informed large parts of our lives and now we were at the beginnings of a relationship that we now know has spanned many lifetimes. We have both had many experiences of our past lives and our past loves – we are twin souls destined to find each other, not just to rekindle a love of ages but for us to inspire our purposes here, in these bodies at this time. We know we are both here to serve others, to help them awaken, and to help them heal and realise the greatest and most loving gifts they have are who they are on the inside.

The most beautiful of events that has happened so far in our relationship was my sudden realisation of who Krista was to me and why I was so drawn to her, why she could melt me with just a hello. During one of the meditations that helped me recover more of my NDE, I had a realisation – It hit me like the freight train that hit her when she viewed my video post on Facebook. Krista – she was my angel lady. She came to ask me to come and find her. In those moments of deep meditation, she became the ocean of love that had washed over me. I'd always been drawn to Krista's presence, her smile, the voice that can turn me into a hot melted puddle, and now I knew why. Then everything else made sense. All the spontaneous regressions we had. The healing we had caused in each other. The intense magnetic draw, of my heart to hers. All the synchronicities that to this day continue to work their magic to keep us forging forward.

It has been written about in many forms, in many languages and over many generations and lifetimes – synchronicities. They constantly occur but are rarely noticed in any present moment, rather they are marveled at from the perspective of hindsight. I am drawn to write about them here as I pull together the now complete recollection of my near death experience.

I want to express it here because despite how we may feel about our lives, there is a plan and we are integral parts. We are here to experience aspects of the divine that we are born from, each of us bringing something special to the table, something that no one else can bring. We are all needed for the evolution of the collective and to fulfill the divine plan that we all agreed to. It is hard sometimes from an individual perspective to see our own purpose in that plan, especially if we cringe at what we have been, or wince when we become aware of the "negative" effect we seem to have had on those around us.

This is all part of the plan and as dualistic beings we often need the contrast to move "forward," so here, right now, I want anyone reading or hearing these words to stop, just for a moment and realise that everything is perfect and had to happen in the way it happened to bring us all to this moment. What happens after this now is completely up to us. We can't fail, whatever it is that we decide to do.

We are at our most powerful and most wonderful when we are present in any moment, this is never more potent than when we own our choices and in turn own the situations we find ourselves in. We have created and co-created our ways through life and everything that we have experienced up to this point is down to a choice that we have made. The choices that help us create our lives come in a number of parts: Firstly, there's the ultimate creational choice and that's called the soul's choice. Before we incarnate into any lifetime – we choose what it is that we want to experience; we choose who we want to be and what events we want to create which would help us to achieve the goals of that experience. Next, we also choose who we want to help us achieve these things, and this covers every conceivable eventuality. Even as I write this I am being given information about how we choose all the souls that we want to experience this life with, to cover all possibilities – we even choose souls that may or may not take an active part in our lives.

To help us get from start point A (which is when we are born) to end point B (which is when we go home) we have predestined events lined up and predestined souls who will enter our lives, too. Now because we have free will to choose what we think and feel in any given moment, we also have the choice to create and co-create based on our continued vibrational output. On this basis alone it would be easy to conceive that we could have a predestined plan at point A and go way off course by the time we get to point B.

So how is it possible that life, regardless it seems of choice, happens in exactly the way it was always meant to and how does it not interfere with our creational abilities within the free will that we are given? This is where synchronicity really shines through and where certain events or souls seems to magically appear – just at the right time to nudge us along. These nudges come in all forms both "negative" and "positive." I can most definitely attest to this and I want now to share part of my earthly experience as an example.

So you see, the universe is indeed clever. The real beauty of its intelligence is the very loving way that we are integral parts of its inner workings. We are the players in this game, and although humanly it can seem like we just wing it – when it comes to living, there is a divine order, a purpose to everything. Every breath we take carries the plan to perfection – and not just the plan for the individual, but for the collective. Not just for the collective, but the planet. Not just the planet, but the universe as a whole. I think about this every time I start to punish myself for all the things I'm still not proud of. I don't think I'll ever be proud of everything, but I accept that I was only a part of each of those scenarios, that the pebbles that were dropped caused ripples – ripples upon ripples that have been chosen as necessary and part of the plan.

Where I have felt guilty for being the cause for so much of the upset when I was still with my ex, I now see the plan – I see that we both chose to play these parts so that we could be who we are now and interact with who we are with now. It is not just me who is divinely happy and healing, she is on her path, too. Being a person within herself who is happier and more self-assured.

This has been the driving force for me and in her way for Krista, too. We both realised that our greatest gifts have always been the love that we can show to ourselves. A large portion of our path together has brought waves of healing that have at times left us drowning. In those moments, we have realised that we were only drowning to our old selves, we were merely shedding layers that we no longer needed, and each time we have emerged like beautiful butterflies beating our wings on the winds of love.

These times have helped us to also help others. We have been gifted with a number of wonderful occasions where we have been able to share our experiences and our love. We have seen the healing energy of our stories enliven people by helping them to see that they deserve that level of love too, not just from others or from the outer universe, but from themselves – from their hearts, creating and recreating that heaven that dwells in all of us.

I know you can find this love within you, too. Through my experience, I remembered this love dwells within and is the makeup of every soul and the driving force of our lives, creating and recreating that heaven that dwells within all of us. Thank you for taking the time to read my story.

About Ainsley

Ainsley Threadgold has been a police officer since 2005. He currently lives in the UK and is in the middle of writing a book with his full story, which he hopes to finish and publish in 2018. In 2015 he met the love of his life Krista, who also experienced an NDE. During the summer of 2016 he shared a stage with Krista at the IANDS conference (International Association for Near Death Studies) in Orlando, Florida.

His public Facebook page is the same title as the book he has written: 'Come and Find Me – Life Times of Love.' Ainsley and Krista also share a webpage called buggielove.com. The site's main characters, Buggie and friends, have a simple but profound message dedicated to love and acceptance of all.

Heaven is Empty
Wisdom From The Other Side

Yvonne Ballard

I am very honored and grateful that you have chosen to spend some time with me. I imagine you want to know how I ended up dead? Well, although it is not an exciting story, it might be a cautionary tale for you. I was a single mother of two teenagers living in a large, expensive American city with very little support. For 10 years, I worked 14-hr days with few days off. I barely slept as a result of working both day and night shifts and I had a horrible diet. Due to an unbearable amount of stress I developed a duodenal ulcer. Lacking health insurance, I tried to heal myself through dietary changes and stress reduction. As hard as I tried, my attempts were not enough.

I eventually developed pneumonia due to a compromised immune system coupled with working around ill people. I still couldn't afford to get medically treated and the pneumonia got progressively worse. The pneumonia though is not what caused my death. My ulcer perforated, which means that there was a hole from my small bowel into the sterile part of my abdominal cavity. Very quickly my body went into septic shock and I was found lifeless on the floor next to my bed. I was rushed to the hospital and little did I know how much my life was about to change. Now here is where the fun begins!

After dying, the first thing I remember is looking down on my body from the ceiling and watching the excellent work of the emergency team as they tried to save my life. I watched for a while out of curiosity and felt satisfied that they were doing a good job, so I moved on. I felt no fear, only relief and excitement! I did not see a tunnel or light, as I have now come to know they are reserved for reincarnated beings. I am an incarnated being, meaning this is my first time on Earth, therefore I had no tunnel or light to go through. During this time, I kept being drawn to people who were thinking of me. I was 48 years old and too young to be dying. So many people were sad and worried. Every time anyone started to think about me, I was standing right next to them. To me, we were both as physical and real as I am today, but they couldn't see me. It would take me a split second to remember that they couldn't see me and I would go. Please remember this the next time you think of a loved one who has passed on. Simply think of them, and they will be standing right by your side sending you their love!

Next, I recall having a life review, even though I wouldn't name it this and use this term only for your reference. From my perspective, I saw my life but it wasn't linear, it was all at once. In one moment, I thought/saw/felt/read my entire existence and I saw how my life contributed to the whole. I experienced being a part of the multiverse and how it morphed and changed with my slightest thought and deed. I did not see my or anyone's actions as good or bad. All I saw were the beautiful creations that occurred because of us. My childhood, much like a kaleidoscope, formed beautiful designs with every movement.

What I realized is that before you come here you have a basic plan that doesn't change. Think of your life as a puzzle broken up into a million pieces and thrown out into the time/space continuum. You have free will to decide how you will complete the puzzle, but the picture that is your life will not change. Your free will is that you can relax, live in joy and happiness easily flowing from piece to piece or you can live in anger and fear struggling to find each piece. There is no right or wrong way to do it. All experiences are valid. Many reincarnated beings want to experience extreme low vibrations of war, death, disease, control and destruction. Other beings want to experience high vibrations of peace, love and harmony. All experiences are valid and all beings choose. There are no victims. We are all Creator Gods. Refrain from judgment because you don't know what kind of life an entity chose to experience. The only thing you can control and your only job is you! Of course you can help people if it makes you feel good, but do so with no expectation.

The next thing I saw were many, many people dying and going to their respective heavens and hells. The people who thought they deserved to go to hell created horrible places full of demons with people crying and wailing in agony. These places were straight out of the scariest verses in the Bible. Quickly these entities realized they didn't have to stay there and moved on. Funny enough, they didn't move on as fast as the people who had created classic heavens. The heaven people created beautiful cities of gold, silver and diamonds. Blue skies were filled with far off angels singing melodious hymns. The heaven people would sometimes walk the glittering streets with Jesus or Mother Mary. Occasionally Jehovah God sat smiling on the throne in the cloud. The heaven people though most frequently walked on the glittering streets alone. They thought God would take care of all the details, so they were left alone with nothing to do and very uncomfortable. Needless to say, they left the fastest. People who stayed the longest in their paradise were the ones who created natural settings. They were frequently alone just relaxing and at peace.

As I pulled back further, I suddenly understood the illusion of time. I remember saying to myself, "Oh yeah! Now I remember!" I struggled at this point to remember how time worked. Before I go any further, I would like to answer a frequently asked question. Why are near death experience stories so different? People create NDE's for many reasons. You have to understand that from your perspective as a human living in time/space, it seems like dying is a huge jump. In reality it is no different from taking a breath or stepping through a doorway. I had a NDE because I was so far off my path that it was the best way for me to remember why I came. Someone else may have one because they have what is considered an evil life and they have a NDE to see Jesus or God to then come back as a fervent born again Christian. Perspectives also differ based on what one's interests are. The other side is a very big place and not everyone is going to be drawn to the same thing. You see it is all about experience and perspective. We are all Creator Gods. We create, we experience then we create some more.

Okay, so back to where I remembered the illusion of time. As I pulled back further, I felt what others have described as unconditional love, however this feeling went way beyond that. Excuse the graphic nature of this content, but the feeling was like that moment of pure ecstasy when you and your lover climax at the same time and all energies are one - body, mind and soul! That moment of ecstasy is what I felt all of the time. It was the merging of all beings in perfect oneness. No wonder why

I was not happy to come back! From here on I knew everything about everything. This will sound strange to you, but everyone knew everything there. I could read, feel and interpret vibrations. The vibrations had all the information. I could narrow my focus like a microscope and know what the experience was of a single atom in the wing of a fly or pull back and know the experience of the multiverse. I zoomed around visiting billions and billions of perspectives for what seemed like decades. Then I remember thinking that I should go back to Earth and do something. Immediately I woke up in the hospital and I couldn't remember why I had come back. What I did remember immediately was that I was stuck back in time and space. Inside I silently screamed, "Oh no, no, no...I want to go home! I don't want to be back here!"

I cried as the physical pain crept into my awareness. At this point, I had no idea I had been in intensive care for almost a month. My kids were standing at my bedside looking terrified. As most nurses do, I taught my children to never put me on any life-saving machines. Well, they had put me on all of them. After the doctors took me off the machines, they told the kids I would probably not wake up. When I woke up they told the kids I would probably be severely cognitively impaired. They said that if I weren't cognitively impaired I would surely never walk again because of the damage to my heart by the bacterial infection. The doctors continued by saying to my children that if I managed to walk again, I would certainly never be able to work. Needless to say, that was my worst fear – being helpless. My children knew this and were afraid that I would be furious. I don't know why. I never paid much attention to the doctors my whole nursing career and this would be no exception.

Being the stubborn person I am, I immediately tried to get out of bed to go to the bathroom and fell flat on my face. I knew right then and there that there was more to the story. The kids quickly told me the story on this side of the veil and I knew this wasn't going to be easy. I did not want to be back and during the struggle of the next year and a half my thoughts frequently turned to how I could get home again. I couldn't walk, my memory was fuzzy and I was a single mom who had been in a coma for a month without insurance. I had children to care for, no place to live, no money, very little support and I was on medication of $50 a day. No problem, right?

I begged for help and got a place to stay. Then I started researching home remedies to replace the medication. I also started building up my strength mostly by very, very slowly mowing the lawn.

Eventually I got my strength back and healed myself using herbs and by detoxifying my system. Within a year and a half I was working full time again. Unfortunately, my healing process had made me acutely aware that most of my nursing career I had inadvertently done harm to people. I had so wanted to help and this knowledge ate me up. I couldn't take it anymore, so I saved a few thousand dollars and bought a 25-ft travel trailer and decided to travel. Well, that isn't the whole truth. What I really wanted was to buy a sailboat and sail the world. My daughter was not thrilled with the idea as she had too much stuff and a cat. Of course she did have a point as I had never been on a sailboat nor did I know how to sail, so we compromised on the travel trailer. I didn't know how I was going to make money, but I knew my daughter and I would at least have a roof over our heads.

Time passed and although I have never forgotten one tiny aspect of my time on the other side, I do figure out how to explain it more efficiently and effectively every day. So that is the basic story and now for the fun part. I am going to choose a few things to tell you that I remember from the other side. I am going to choose some things I am frequently asked and other things I have not been asked and answer those questions from a different perspective. That's what everything is about – perspective and experience.

One of the most asked questions is why do we come here if it is so nice over there? Well, everyone comes for their own reason. Many simply come to experience the lower vibrations available only in the third dimension. Earth specifically has the most complete array of 3D vibrations available. You would interpret those vibrations as emotions. There are planets in the multiverse that have a few emotions both on the good end as well as the bad, but on Earth they are all here. There are many of us who came here to help the planet transition into 5D. There are some who came just to check it out for a single incarnation while others have reincarnated thousands of times. There is no single reason why beings come to this time and place. What is important to remember is that there is no one reason and no right way. Everyone has their reasons and all reasons are not only valid but also important and special to the whole.

Is there a God? Yes, there are many gods and goddesses, but let's back up a little before everyone freaks out. There is an entity that I will call the Creator that came up with the idea to create a multiverse based on light/dark and duality. Others with him came up with the idea of amnesia making is so that when you come here you would not remember who you

184

truly are. The entity that came up with the light/dark concept is no different than you and me. We have all created things this complex. When he came up with this idea, the Creator decided to keep track of the light side of the game. He then asked for a volunteer to handle the dark side. This was a big task because the dark side has the lower vibrations and going that low is difficult. A great friend of the Creator volunteered to handle the dark side. This is whom must humans identify as Lucifer. So, at the very top is Source, which is all things. Then within that is the Creator and Lucifer. Then within that creation there are many gods and goddesses who have been created over time - the Greek, Roman and Egyptian gods and goddesses as well as Jehovah and Satan. These facts do not invalidate anyone's religious beliefs except to show that everyone is on their own path for their own reasons. We must allow this, support each other, trust each other and not judge or interfere. When we understand and live with these principles we will be free of fear and be able to experience the 5th dimension.

What should we be eating? The first and most important step is to detoxify. It is better for the human body to not eat anything that is processed. I'm a huge supporter of the Farmer's Market. If you can grow or raise your own food, that is best. It is very important for us to understand that as long as we are eating, something has to die for us to live. Those beings that you are eating, no matter how careful you are, will have a certain amount of fear. This includes plants. Somehow we have gotten into this meat vs. vegan debate and one of the main issues is the hurting of animals. People think that just animals hurt, but plants and anything with a seed also feel fear. So what to do? Again, you must first detoxify your system. You can go online and find hundreds of detoxifying regimes. Just pick the one you like. Next, clean food, water and juices. Next, go old school and pause before taking anything into your body and thank it from your whole heart for giving its life to you. Thank the people who prepared it. Thank the people who cared for the plant or animal. Thank the people who transported the plant or animal to you. Thank the people who sold it to you. Become very aware of what it takes to feed you. Your high vibrations filled with love and appreciation will alter the food and in turn provide sustenance for your body that will allow it to heal and thrive.

Another vital step to healing and thriving is to utilize pranic breathing. As a Creator God, you have access to everything your body needs directly from Source. Sun gazers and breatharians use pranic breathing to draw energy into their bodies. This is much more efficient than taking in food and breaking it down into energy. By doing this we can stop eating plants and animals. This will reduce the fear vibrations on the planet and greatly and substantially help in getting us firmly into the 5th dimension.

Since nursing is my forte, let's go further into health and disease. Let's be very clear. With the right support your body will never be sick. With the right support your body can heal anything. With the right support, your body ages very, very slowly or not at all. So why do we live in a world that has so much death and disease? Well, the short answer is we wanted it this way. When planets, including Earth, are set up for entities to experience lower vibrations, the planet has to have bad things happening to elicit those low vibrations. Low vibrations include despair, fear and anger. Animals are hunted and killed to set up an environment of fear. Plants are grown and consumed for the same reason. Modern systems are built on competition, which instills fear. Religions, schools, businesses and governments are all built on rules and these rules lead to worry which is fear. Fear leads to an inability to relax or sleep. Relaxation, deep breathing and sleep are the very best ways to allow healing energy into your body. Insomnia and stress are linked to every single disease. So how do you heal? Again, detoxify your food and detoxify your life. To stay healthy, you must disengage from the old food and ways to find a new path. You must trust yourself and your body. Become crazy protective and responsible for your own well being. This includes heart, mind, body and soul.

I was raised to follow the rules. I was told that I should work hard and I would succeed. This is NOT correct as we head into the 5th dimension. You should not work at all let alone hard. You should do what you love. There will be people who love to fix cars. There will be people who love to build houses. There will be people who love to clean. Everything that needs doing will be done including what you would consider the bad stuff. To get there, everyone needs to figure out what they truly love and do it. We are going to have to stop doing what other people want us to do because this causes disease and death. The Earth we are heading to has no death. We will stay as long as we like in time/space then simply leave when we are ready.

I know that right now in 2017 it looks chaotic, but it really is not. It is all progressing beautifully. People are waking up fast. People are developing psychic powers fast. We are finding out that ADHD and autistic people are actually geniuses. The children are being born with little to no amnesia so they can impart wisdom and help the transformation into the 5th dimension. Many, many people are connecting with their higher selves. We are listening and learning. People are looking at the world around them and opting to change in big ways. Because of this, old systems are breaking down. That is the way it has to be, so don't be afraid. This is a great thing. There is and will be plenty to replace those old systems. If you knew how much help this planet is getting in this process you really wouldn't worry. There are so many lovely alien beings helping us all right now and I want to tell them that I am so very thankful for their support and assistance.

Now, just a little thought about the Internet. There have been some complaints that people are isolating themselves, especially the young people. Please don't worry about this. The Internet is the preamble to telepathy. We are getting used to being open and honest with each other. First anonymously, then openly. It is connecting all kinds of different people around the world with different viewpoints. It is teaching us to empathize and understand one another. The Internet has massive information available and this teaches us to easily and quickly access data and use it. This is preparing us to access what some people call The Akashic Records. The healers can reach through the Internet and teach everyone to self-heal. The psychics can reach through the Internet and teach psychic abilities to everyone. The telekinetics can reach through the Internet and teach telekinesis to everyone. The autistic can reach through the Internet and teach humans the new way to perceive and collect huge blocks of data. The new way will be to share what you are experiencing and what you can do, no matter where you are on your journey.

Before, only enlightened people were deemed special enough to share their wisdom, but that is no longer the way. Now we each have a piece to the puzzle. What is happening to you in this moment is important. Speak your truth every day. Sure, there will be people who make fun of you in the moment, but something you say might help them look at something differently when they need it. Keep being true to yourself. Don't judge yourself or others. The others are Creator Gods just like you. Trust that they have a planned path and they know what they are doing even though it may not look like it to you in the moment.

I have tried to explain why bad things happen so you can see there is a plan. Now, as things transition you have a choice on what to watch and give your time and energy to. There are wondrous events happening every day. There are also horrifyingly scary things happening everyday as the old systems die. Which will you watch? I suggest the wondrous events. It is so much more fun!

Now let's talk about good and bad. From the Creator's standpoint, vibrations were divided into two major groups. The higher vibrations identified as light and good. The lower vibrations identified as dark and bad. We cannot have this whole creation without both sides. Both sides are necessary for the 3rd dimensional experience! Therefore, we have needed entities playing at both sides for this creation to work. Over the last few decades there has been a lot of discussion on "Service to Others" vs. "Service to Self". During this time, the "Service to Others" energy level has increased and that is wonderful. However, I want people to understand that "Service to Others" is in the same category as "Service to Self." No one serves others unless it feels good, therefore it is a service to self to serve others. The reason why this is important is it is a step toward unity consciousness. When we accept all people and all paths and when we serve others and ourselves with no judgment or expectations, we are well on our way to unity consciousness. Unity consciousness leads us to the 5th dimension and the 5th dimension is wonderful!

So what about the magical beings and extinct or near extinct fish and animals? I know these do not seem to go together, but they do. Magical beings especially fairies, are frequently seen by children and animals. They are all still here, they just exist on a different frequency. It's kind of like looking through ultraviolet lenses. You see things through ultraviolet lenses that you cannot see with your bare eyes. If you had magical lenses you would see the magical beings too. Like aliens, magical beings, animals and marine life know how to change their vibrations and become invisible to humans. As we increase our vibration, we will be able to see all these beings and interact with them again. These beings are waiting for us with so much excitement! This is especially true with the fairies as they LOVE, LOVE, LOVE humans and have really missed us as we dropped to the lower vibrations. So keep your eyes open for more whales, dolphins, aliens, and all sorts of magical beings!

So how many of you are asking, what happened to Yvonne? What are you doing now? Am I alright? Well, after I bought the travel trailer, my daughter and I stayed in a couple of RV parks as I continued to work in nursing to save money. We didn't care for that much so we started staying in state and national parts for two weeks at a time. When I had saved about $6,000, which was enough to keep us going for a year, I retired from nursing. We wandered around just relaxing in nature and meeting wonderful people. Eventually we rented a small farm in the Hill Country of Texas. There was a horrible fire and many horses were just dumped by the side of the road because people couldn't afford to feed them. We started to find them and then fattened them up, retrained them and found them new homes. When we got to about 10 horses we started a trail riding business. This was a great hit and wonderful fun. Unfortunately, the place we were renting decided to sell the property for $750,000 and we had to move.

I looked everywhere but there was nothing that was appropriate that we could afford. I started looking further away and found a farm for rent in North East Texas that was big enough for our menagerie. I found homes for as many horses as I could and moved five of them. When we got here we found out the trail riding business was not an option. We then opened a micro green business and sold to high-end restaurants in Dallas. In the meantime this property, which has two houses, came up for sale. The wonderful owners sold it to us with no credit check and no down payment. We then rented one of the houses and live in the other. The microgreen business has died as the economy died. We now live solely on the rental property income. My daughter has plans to buy cars that need work, fix them up and custom paint them for women.

I, on the other hand have minimalized my life. Since the near-death experience, I have worked very hard at removing negativity of all kinds from my life. I am selling my travel trailer and then am going to backpack in South America. Eventually, I will also travel the USA, Canada, Alaska and anywhere else in the world I happen to be led. So, if you would like a visitor of if you just want to visit, send me an email at brenballard@yahoo.com. I would love to come and visit you and learn your perspective. I want to give a giant hug and thank you to Karen Swain for reaching out to me. Since our interview, I am much calmer and clearer. That was a huge step for me because I don't talk about all this weird stuff to people. She is such a loving, open person and a fantastic interviewer. So a big, big hug to my friend Down Under!

My final thought for everyone is just to love yourself, love others and love this planet. Everything is going great! Trust yourself! You are exactly where you are supposed to be and you are doing magnificently! Mostly remember you are not alone. You have never been alone! You are a lovely, unique and special person. You are cherished and loved so deeply by so many! Hugs to you all! Joy, light, love and Namaste from your friend Yvonne.

About Yvonne

Yvonne Ballard was born February 8th, 1960 in Laramie, Wyoming, USA. Her family was one of the original ranchers in Wyoming and their family home is now a museum to preserve the history of the Northern Wild, Wild West. Yvonne has been married and divorced twice and has two adult children. She is a retired registered nurse with neurological, intensive care and emergency room expertise. Yvonne had her near-death experience at the end of 2008 during a month-long coma. After the coma, it took a year to regain her physical health, but it took another 4 years to interpret what she saw and experienced on the other side. Yvonne now lives in North East Texas and after decades of living in fear, she fervently protects her happiness and practices trust and unconditional love daily. You can find her talking about her near-death experience on her popular YouTube channel under her name 'Yvonne Ballard'.

Bonus Material
Sandra Champlain's 19 Reasons to Believe in Life After Death

This material is researched from Sandra's radio Podcast show. You can find out more at wedontdieradio.com

Evidential Mediums - Like tuning into a radio station, evidential mediums tune into the vibration of our loved ones in the spirit world. I believe we all possess the capability to do this. Becoming a good medium takes work though. It takes dedication, commitment and practice. You don't have to spend a lot of money either. One of my favorite resources is www.snui.org the Spiritualists' National Union. They give several free readings at the end of every service.

Spirit Artists - are mediums who draw. Reverend Rita Berkowitz (now retired) www.thespiritartist.com has many photographs and portraits on her website of the spirit people she has seen. After my dad passed, Rita drew a portrait of my father how he appeared in in his 20's and told me we all get to be our favorite age in the hereafter. With no artistic abilities, she will go into a trance-like state, and a spirit artist named Leo uses her hands to draw pictures of those in the spirit world. She has been filmed drawing two different portraits at the same time, one with her left hand and one with her right!

IADC - Induced After Death Communication and Grief Reattachment Therapy - both Allan Botkin and Rochelle Wright have perfected methods to induce after death communication between you and a loved one. It is a timely procedure for those intensely grieving. Using counseling and EMDR (Eye Movement Desensitization and Reprocessing), therapists effectively move you into a state of mind where you may talk and touch your loved ones.

Death Bed Visitations - Just before death we often hear of people looking up, seeing and talking to those in Heaven. I especially love the stories of people who have been in a coma, not knowing their friends had passed away, then they see them in a death bed visitation! Dr. Penny Sartori, Dr, Pam Kircher and hospice chaplain Steve Kearney have some great stories. As a couple of famous examples, Thomas Edison whispered to his physician just before death "It is very beautiful over there." Steve Jobs final words while looking over the shoulders of his family were "Oh Wow. Oh Wow. Oh Wow."

Electronic Voice Phenomena - Using technology we are able to record sounds of raindrops, radio static or other "white noise" and have voices appear when we play it back. I have recorded several hundred of these messages that have been heard by many and are very healing. For my story listen to episode #1 of We Don't Die Radio. Tom Butler and his wife Lisa taught me about EVPs and there is also a lot of fantastic information by Sonia Rinaldi and Sheri Perl.

Visual ITC - (Instrumental Transcommunication) is the practice of recording faces, places and images from the afterlife on photographs and video recordings. Tom Butler, Sonia Rinaldi, Rebecca O'Donnell and Keith Clark have great stories of what they have captured with visual ITC. Visit www.atransc.org.

Heaven talks to Children - When our minds are young and not fully developed very often we can see "beyond the veil" into the other side. Children have told parents who they see, and they are just as real to them as alive human beings. Parents are mystified that these children often know names and descriptions of people that they have never heard about. Christine Duminiak has written a book on this subject that you can check out, and psychic medium Leo Bonomo clearly remembers his childhood visitations.

Guardian Angels and Spirit Guides - It is very comforting to believe that we have invisible souls looking after us while we are on earth. It is also said that we work with these beings to choose the life we wish to live and the experiences / life lessons we wish to have. Lorna Byrne has been seeing angels since childhood. They have communicated with her and taught very profound things. Different mediums have described the same Spirit Guides around people and have stepped in to help us in times of need. I've heard stories of peoples' lives being saved by these helpers, only to find out that no person was physically there.

Reincarnation - Dr. Ian Stevenson spent his life interviewing and documenting the stories of over three-thousand children around the world who possessed memories from their past lives—and that included discovering physical evidence of the past lives such as birthmarks. I am grateful to have interviewed Susan Masino who tells the story of her very young son having nightmares of dying on a sinking ship. His drawings were replicas of the ship Titanic, a blueprint of the ship complete with the stairwells and layout of the actual vessel.

NDE (Near Death Experiences) - have been documented by millions of people worldwide. While their experiences can greatly differ, there are some similarities. These may include moving toward a bright light, the feeling of unconditional love, seeing relatives and having a life review. While our skeptical mind often listens to the argument that it's all part of our brain shutting down before death, the stories of NDE survivors can be shocking. Blind people who have never seen with their human eyes have accurately "seen" events that have taken place in hospitals, and people remember their NDEs clearer than any other memory they have had. All those I've spoken with now have no fear of dying and make their lives about helping others. Dr. Penny Sartori, scientist Nancy Rynes and Dr. Mary Neal are a few of my favourite NDE guests.

OBE (Out of Body Experiences) - are similar to the NDE, however you don't have to be near death to have one. Through meditation and practices we have the opportunity to see into Heaven. Author Cyrus Kirkpatrick, Sean McNamara and Luis Minero share some fabulous stories on OBEs.

Shared Death Experiences - Similar to NDEs, loved ones of people transitioning often share the experiential journey into the Hereafter. They can see, hear and feel what their loved one is experiencing as their bodies die. Dr. Raymond Moody, who coined the term "Near Death Experience" has a wonderful book called "Glimpses of Eternity: An Investigation Into Shared Death Experiences" talks about his work .

Life Between Lives & Past Lives - Dr. Brian Weiss, author "Many Lives, Many Masters" has done much work in the field of survival of the human soul. During hypnotic regression, people have experienced who they were in past lives. Dr. Michael Newton, author of "Journey of Souls" offers excellent evidence that our consciousness survives physical death. Currently past life / between life therapies are available for people. Dr. Ann Clark discusses this in more detail.

Trance Mediums - are people that go into a deep meditative state and blend their energy with the energy of a deceased person. While there are many types of trance mediums, I have personally witnessed three:

1) Trance speaking: a different personality than the person in trance speaks through the mouth of the medium. The messages are filled with inspiration and often poetic about love, life and the afterlife.

2) Trance Communication: a person's deceased loved one actually uses the medium's mouth to speak, having a conversation with their loved one face to face, similar to Patrick Swayze's character using Whoopi Goldberg's character to speak in the movie "Ghost."

3) Trance writing: with the medium in a trance state, he or she may draw, write poetry or words of inspiration or write in the hand-writing of someone's deceased loved one.

Physical Mediums & Apports - Back in the old days, people would speak of seances, levitations and deceased people appearing real within a cloth-like substance called ectoplasm. While certainly there are many frauds who prey on the grieving, there are some current physical mediums who have mind-blowing stories. I have witnessed "the impossible" myself and do believe in it. One example of physical mediumship phenomena are apports—where objects appear out of nowhere (materialize). For example, a newly printed newspaper from the 1940s appeared in a seance room in the 1990s. It was inspected and proved to be legitimate. Coins, jewelry and more have appeared out of thin air. Scott Milligan, Nic Whitham, Robin Foy, Karl Jackson-Barnes, and Physicist Jan Vandersande have jaw-dropping stories of physical mediumship.

Precipitation Mediumship - is a form of physical mediumship however it is unique. Blank cards, white pieces of fabric or simply a blank canvas may be present before sitting with a medium. Faces of your loved ones and messages often appear on these objects at the end of the meeting. Reverend Kevin Lee is passionate about this type of mediumship. I interviewed him about his journey.

Miracle Healings - are just that, miraculous. I believe they are proof that we are so much more than just bodies. Author Anita Moorjani was cured of cancer while on her deathbed and promised she'd tell her story of the afterlife in exchange for being healed. Alex Hermosillo now helps others heal after his NDE. Bryan Basket and Chris Ratter are different kinds of healers both using energy from the spirit world. Absolutely fascinating!

Signs - We all wish to have some sort of proof that our loved ones live on. Medium Susanne Wilson talks about how our loved ones learn to communicate with us in the "Halls of Reunion." Manipulating energy is not an easy thing and must be learned. Also, we must have positive energy to help our loved ones. To ask for signs, quiet you mind, have faith you are communicating with them even though you can't see them, and listen. You may see lights flicker or the television turn on and off, or you may hear messages in music or a favorite song you shared suddenly comes on the radio. You may find coins or feathers or have butterflies or birds come close. Another manifestation is loved ones may enter your dreams. I do believe we also must talk to our loved ones in spirit first and help them know how to communicate. Ask for the signs we wish to have then expect them and watch for them.

Faith - Simply have faith that the afterlife is real. Most of the world's religions believe in the afterlife and you can too. Have faith that life after death is real, you will see your loved ones again and that your life is for a purpose. With faith you can go after your dreams, be courageous, make a difference for other people in their journeys and rest assured that when you close your eyes on earth that final time, there will be a welcoming committee to great you, love you, embrace you and welcome you Home.

Finally, I want to provide one more resource that I hope will help you. When I was experiencing so much grief, as I discussed in my chapter, I realized grief is painful enough. We don't have to lose our relationships over it. So I took all the information I gathered about grief, including what things we can do to ease the pain. I created a 70 minute audio called "How to Survive Grief." You can hear it on my website survivegrief.com. I shared it with my friends and within a few months noticed it had been downloaded over three thousand times! Emails started flooding into my mailbox. Not only did people say their pain had lessened, but people told me they did not commit suicide because of the information this provided.

Thank you for buying this book.

Did you enjoy it?
If so, please join the discussion on our Facebook page and Facebook group at the; Awakening Empowerment Network
www.facebook.com/groups/AwakeningEmpowermentNetwork

Also, please remember to leave a review on Amazon, this will greatly help us spread the word. Thank You.

Find More Stories of Transformation at
theawakeningsoulseries.com

BIG LOVE

Made in the USA
Coppell, TX
05 June 2022